PASSION

AWAKENING

editor **ANDREW HIGH**
art design **MARC LUDENA**
production coordinator **LIZ GEORGE**
executive producer **JOHN J. THOMPSON**

WORSHIP TOGETHER.com®

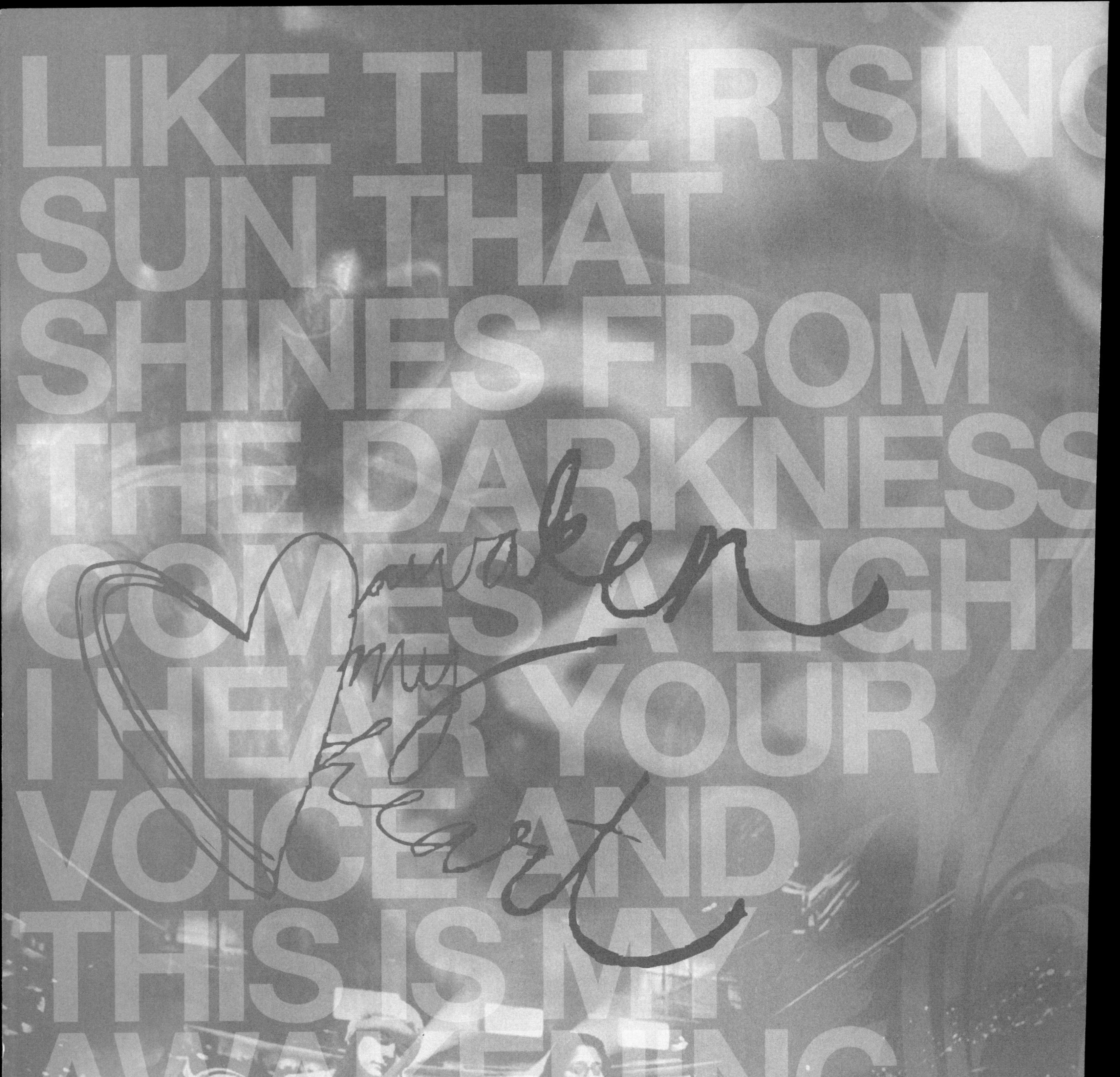
LIKE THE RISING
SUN THAT
SHINES FROM
THE DARKNESS
COMES A LIGHT
I HEAR YOUR
VOICE AND
THIS IS MY
AWAKENING
awaken
my
heart

TABLE OF CONTENTS

LIKE THE RISING
SUN THAT
SHINES FROM
THE DARKNESS
COMES A LIGHT
I HEAR YOUR
VOICE AND
THIS IS MY
AWAKENING

Awakening

Words and Music by
CHRIS TOMLIN and
REUBEN MORGAN

11
B♭(add4)
(A(add4))
Spir - it, we de - sire
mo - ment, in this hour,
13
A♭
(G)
E♭maj7
(Dmaj7)
mf
a - wak - en - ing.
a - wak - en - ing.
For You, and You
CHORUS
16
A♭2(no3)
(G2(no3))
Cm7
(Bm7)
a - lone a - wake my soul; a - wake
mf
18
E♭2(no3)
(D2(no3))
B♭
(A)
my soul, and sing. For the world

20
A♭2(no3) (G2(no3))
Cm7 (Bm7)
E♭2(no3) (D2(no3))
__ You love Your will __ be done, let Your will __ be done __ in me. __
23
1. B♭ (A)
p
__ 2. In Your __
2. B♭ (A)
D.S. to CHORUS
__ For You, and You __
26
3. B♭ (A)
A♭ (G)
Fm7 (Em7)
mp
30
Cm7 (Bm7)
E♭2(no3) (D2(no3))
Fm7 (Em7)

33
A♭
(G)
B♭
(A)
f
Like the ris - ing sun
BRIDGE
36
A♭
(G)
that shines,
Fm7
(Em7)
from the dark - ness comes
mf - f
38
Cm7
(Bm7)
a light;
E♭2(no3)
(D2(no3))
I hear Your voice, and
40
Fm7
(Em7)
this is my
A♭
(G)
a - wak - en - ing!

42
1.
Fm7
(Em7)
B♭
(A)
Like the ris - ing sun
2.
44
B♭
(A)
A♭
(G)
Cm7
(Bm7)
ff
48
E♭
(D)
B♭
(A)
A♭
(G)
51
Cm7
(Bm7)
E♭
(D)
B♭
(A)
ff
Like the ris - ing sun

54
A♭ (G)
Cm7 (Bm7)
that shines, a - wake my soul, a - wake
56
E♭ (D)
B♭ (A)
my soul and sing. From the dark - ness comes
Sing 2nd time: On - ly You can raise
58
A♭ (G)
Cm7 (Bm7)
a light; a - wake my soul, a - wake
a life;
60
E♭ (D)
1.
B♭ (A)
my soul and sing. Like the ris - ing sun

Chords Used in This Song

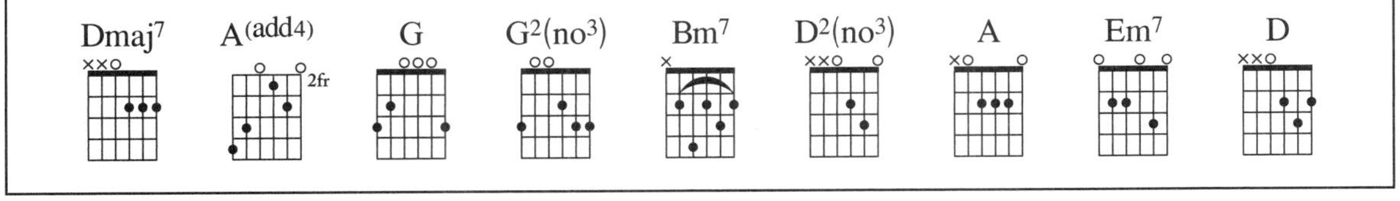

Say Say

Words and Music by
KRISTIAN STANFILL,
CHRIS TOMLIN and CHRISTY NOCKELS

Rock 4 ♩ = 144

9
F
in a ris - en and re - turn - ing King.
12
C
Some are chas - ing the treas - ures of this world;
sim.
14
B♭
we run to a glo - ri - ous re - ward,
16
F
the on - ly name worth liv - ing for!

CHORUS
19
C
f
Say, say! Say, say, say you be-lieve it;
end staccato pattern
22
F2
Am7
sing for the whole world to hear it. We know, and
25
F2
G
we de-clare it: "Je - sus is King!"
28
C
F2
Say, say, say you be-lieve it; sing loud, sing

31
Am7
like you mean it. We know, and we de-clare it:
34
F2
G
2nd time to Coda
C7
"Je - sus is King!" Say, say!
37
VERSE 2
40
C
mf
2. We set our hearts on what will last:
mf

42
B♭
Your Word, Your love, Your faith - ful - ness—
44
F
our hope is built on noth - ing less.
47
C
grad. cresc.
We o - pen wide our mouths to praise.
grad. cresc.
49
B♭
Let this gen - er - a - tion raise
F
a song of free -

52
D.S. al Coda
- dom all our days!
Say, say!
CODA
55
C
B♭
mp
BRIDGE
58
mf C
I be - lieve
Your
61
B♭
C
king - dom come;
the Son of God,

64
B♭
the King of love!
67
C
B♭
I be - lieve
Your king - dom come;
mf
70
F/A
the Son of God,
the
CHORUS
73
B♭
C
ff
King of love!
Say, say, say
ff

76
F2
you be-lieve it; sing for the whole world to hear it.
79
Am7
F2
We know, and we de-clare it: "Je - sus is King!"
82
G
C
Say, say, say you be-lieve it;
85
F2
Am7
sing loud, sing like you mean it. We know, and

Chords Used in This Song

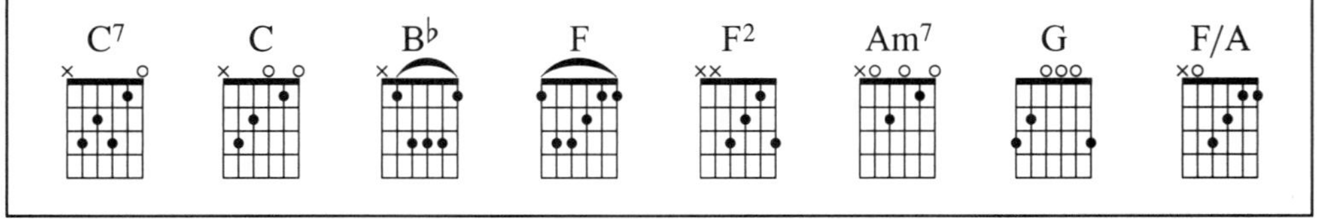

How He Loves

Words and Music by
JOHN MARK McMILLAN

14
G
F2
weight of His wind and mer - cy. And
17
C
all of the sud - den I am un - a - ware of these af -
19
Am7
Gsus
flic - tions e - clipsed by glo - ry; and I real - ize just how
22
G
F2
beau - ti - ful You are, and how great Your af - fec - tions are

CHORUS 1
24
mp
C*
for me.
Oh, how He loves us,
mp
play cued A 2nd time
*Am chord 2nd time
27
Am7
Gsus
oh, oh, how He loves us;
30
G
1.
F2
how He loves us all.
33
2.
F2
C
all.
f

37 Am7 Gsus G
41 F F2 CHORUS 2 C
Yeah, He loves us,
44 Am7 Gsus
O how He loves us, O how He loves us,
48 G F F2
O how He loves! 2. And

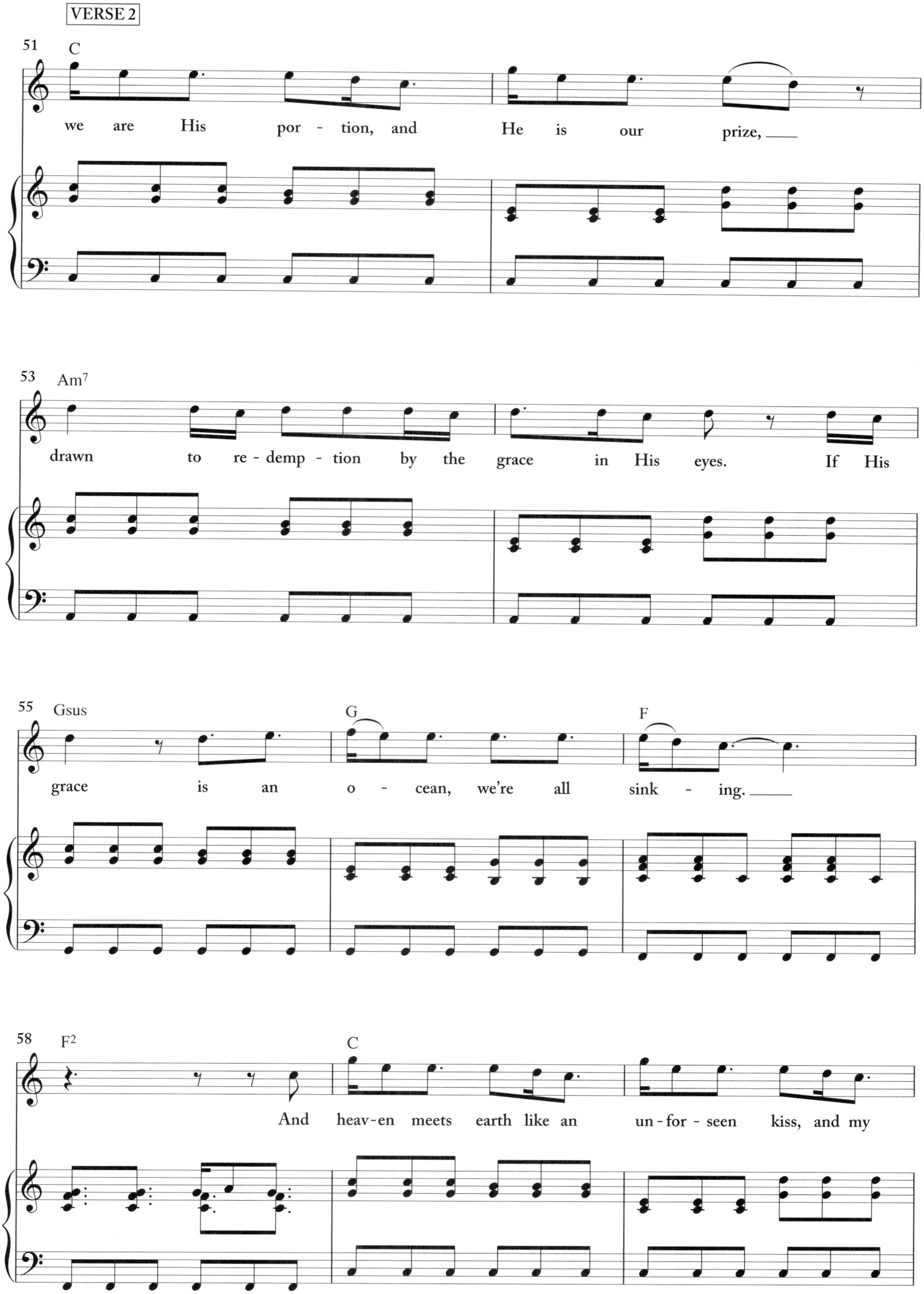
VERSE 2
51
C
we are His por - tion, and He is our prize,
53
Am7
drawn to re - demp - tion by the grace in His eyes. If His
55
Gsus
G
F
grace is an o - cean, we're all sink - ing.
58
F2
C
And heav-en meets earth like an un - for - seen kiss, and my

61
Am7
heart turns vio - lent - ly in - side of my chest; I
63
Gsus
G
don't have time to main - tain these re - grets when I
CHORUS 2
65
F
F2
ff
C
think a - bout the way That He loves us,
ff
68
Am7
O how He loves us, O how He

71 Gsus
G
F
loves us, O how He loves!
74
1. F2
2. F2
C
Yeah, He oh, la la, yeah!
77
Am7
Oh, He loves us all! Oh, how He loves us all!
80 Gsus
G
F
Oh, how He loves us all! Oh, how He loves us

83 F2 p C
all! Yeah, He loves us, O how He
p
86 Am7 Gsus
loves us, O how He loves us,
89 G F F2 C
O how He loves!
93 Am7 Gsus

Chords Used in This Song

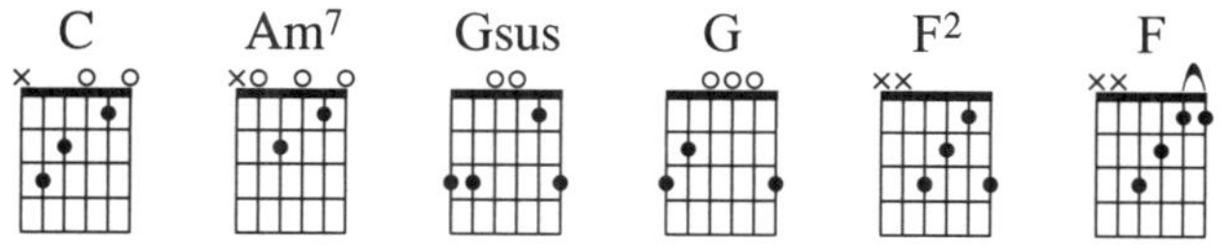

Our God

Words and Music by
MATT REDMAN, JONAS MYRIN,
CHRIS TOMLIN, and JESSE REEVES

Capo 4 (Em)

Moderately ♩ = 105

13
C♯m7
(Am7)
F♯sus
(Dsus)
like You, none like You.
16
F♯
(D)
VERSE 2
mf
G♯m
(Em)
E
(C)
2. In - to the dark - ness, You shine;
18
B
(G)
G♯m
(Em)
E
(C)
out of the ash - es, we rise.
20
B
(G)
C♯m7
(Am7)
There's no one like You, none like

CHORUS
23
F♯sus
(Dsus)
F♯
(D)
G♯m
(Em)
slightly more each time
You.
Our God is great - er,
slightly more each time
L.H. play whole notes 1st time
26
E
(C)
B
(G)
our God is strong - er;
God, You are high - er than an -
28
F♯sus
(Dsus)
G♯m
(Em)
- y oth - er.
Our God is heal - er,
30
E
(C)
B
(G)
awe - some in pow - er, our God,
our God.

32
1.
F♯sus
(Dsus)
G♯m
(Em)
E
(C)
L.H. as written
35
B
(G)
F♯sus
(Dsus)
2.
F♯sus
(Dsus)
D.S. to CHORUS 𝄋
38
3.
F♯sus
(Dsus)
G♯m
(Em)
grad. cresc.
E
(C)
Guitar cues
grad. cresc.
41
B
(G)
F♯sus
(Dsus)
G♯m
(Em)

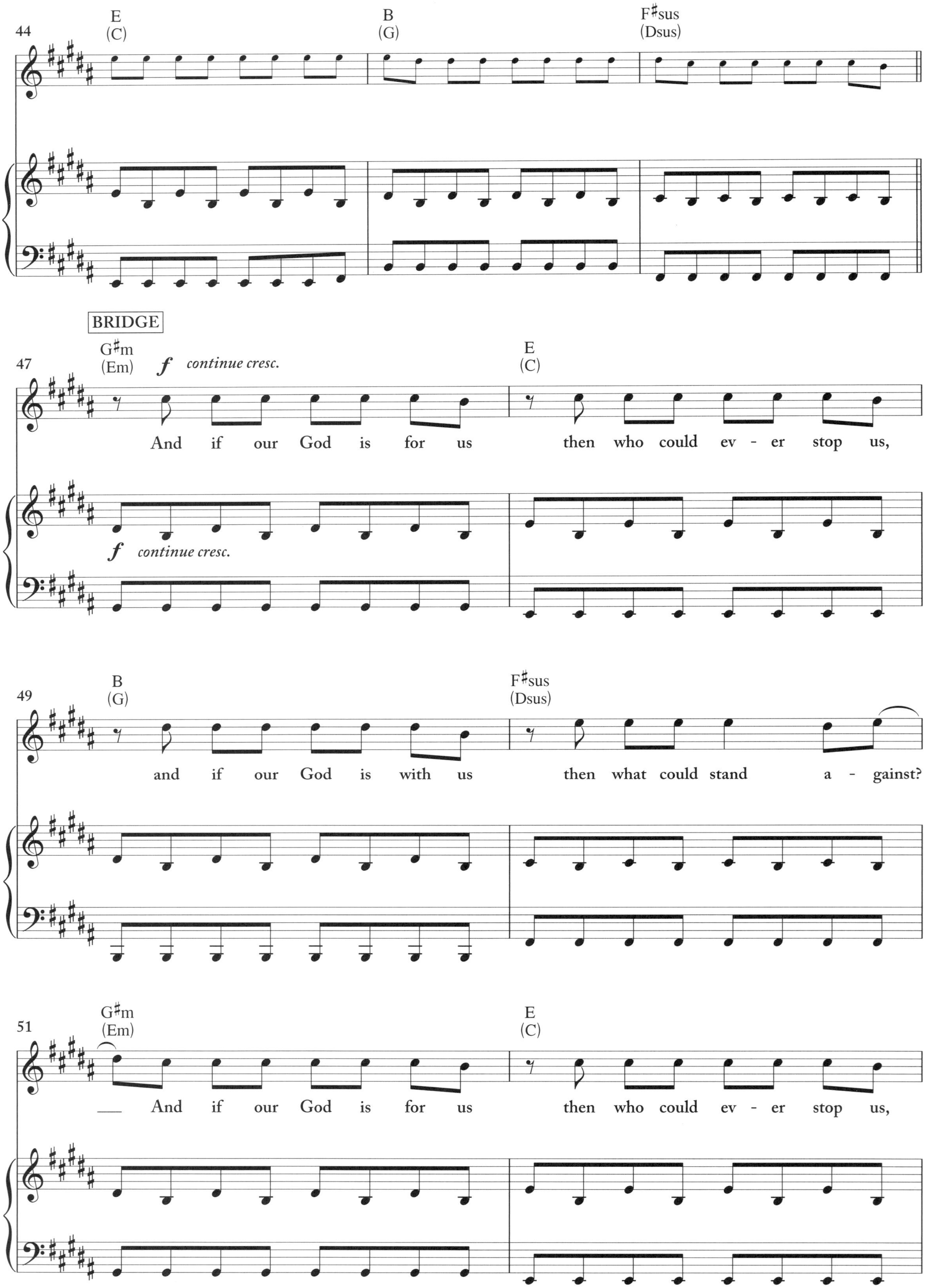
44
E
(C)
B
(G)
F#sus
(Dsus)
BRIDGE
47
G#m
(Em)
f continue cresc.
E
(C)
And if our God is for us then who could ev - er stop us,
f continue cresc.
49
B
(G)
F#sus
(Dsus)
and if our God is with us then what could stand a - gainst?
51
G#m
(Em)
E
(C)
And if our God is for us then who could ev - er stop us,

53
B
(G)
F♯sus
(Dsus)
and if our God is with us then what could stand a - gainst?
55
G♯m
(Em)
ff
E
(C)
B/D♯
(G/B)
58
F♯sus
(Dsus)
G♯m
(Em)
What could stand a - gainst?
60
E
(C)
B/D♯
(G/B)
F♯sus
(Dsus)

CHORUS
63
f
G♯m7(4)
(Em7(4))
E2
(C2)
Our God is great - er, our God is strong - er;
65
B
(G)
F♯/A♯
(D/F♯)
God, You are high - er than an - y oth - er.
67
G♯m7(4)
(Em7(4))
E2
(C2)
Our God is heal - er, awe-some in pow - er, our 3 God,
69
B
(G)
F♯sus
(Dsus)
our 3 God.

BRIDGE
71
G♯m7(4)
(Em7(4))
And if our God is for us
E2
(C2)
then who could ev - er stop us,
73
B
(G)
and if our God is with us
F♯/A♯
(D/F♯)
then what could stand a - gainst? _
75
G♯m7(4)
(Em7(4))
_ And if our God is for us
E2
(C2)
then who could ev - er stop us,
77
B
(G)
and if our God is with us
F♯sus
(Dsus)
then what could stand a - gainst? _

79
G♯m (Em)
ff
E (C)
B/D♯ (G/B)
82
F♯sus (Dsus)
G♯m (Em)
E (C)
Then what could stand a - gainst?
85
B/D♯ (G/B)
F♯sus (Dsus)
poco rit.
CHORUS
88
mp
G♯m7(4) (Em7(4))
Slower
E2 (C2)
Our God is great - er, our God is strong - er;
p
Slower

Chords Used in This Song

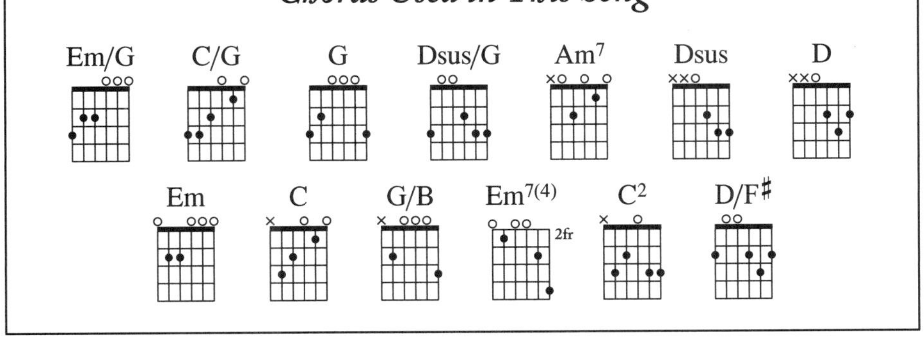

Healing Is in Your Hands

Words and Music by
DANIEL CARSON, CHRISTY NOCKELS,
NATHAN NOCKELS, MATT REDMAN,
and CHRIS TOMLIN

Building steadily throughout ♩ = 86

VERSE 2, 3
11
D
p - mp
D/C♯
Bm7
2. No sick - ness, no se - cret, no chain is
3. Our pres - ent, our fu - ture, our past is
add cued notes 2nd time
14
A
Em7
A
strong e - nough to keep us from Your love, to
in Your hands; we're cov-ered by Your blood, we're
17
Em7
A
mf - f
CHORUS
D
keep us from Your love. How high,
cov-ered by Your blood.
20
A
Bm7
F♯m
how wide; no mat-ter where

23
G2(no3)
D/F♯
F♯m
I am, healing is in Your hands.
26
G2(no3)
D
A
How deep, how strong;
29
Bm7
F♯m
G2(no3)
now by Your grace I stand.
32
D/F♯
F♯m
G2(no3)
Heal-ing is in Your hands.

BRIDGE
D
In all things,
D/C♯
we know that
Bm7
we are more than
A
con - quer - ors; You
Em7
keep us by Your love.
A
D
In all things,
D/C♯
we know that
Bm7
we are more than
A
con - quer - ors; You

47
Em7
cresc.
A
Em7
keep us by Your love.
You keep us by Your love.
cresc.
CHORUS
50
A
ff
D
A
How high,
how wide;
ff
53
Bm7
F♯m
G2(no3)
no mat-ter where I am,
56
D/F♯
F♯m
G2(no3)
heal-ing is in Your hands.
How deep,

Chords Used in This Song

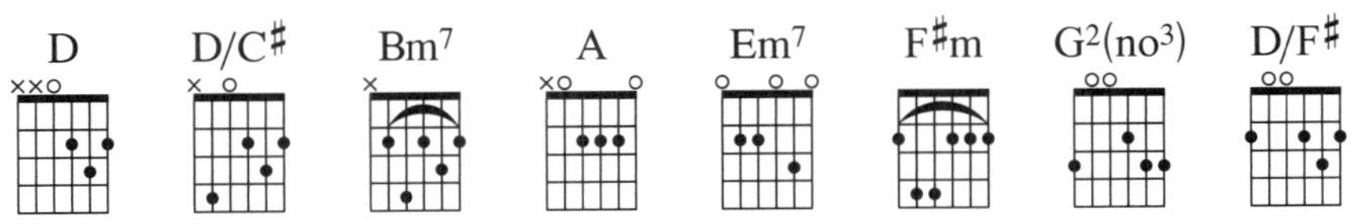

King of Heaven
(Isaiah 61)

Words and Music by
CHARLIE HALL, KENDALL COMBES,
BRIAN BERGMAN, DUSTIN RAGLAND,
and QUINT ANDERSON

With a strong beat ♩ = 132

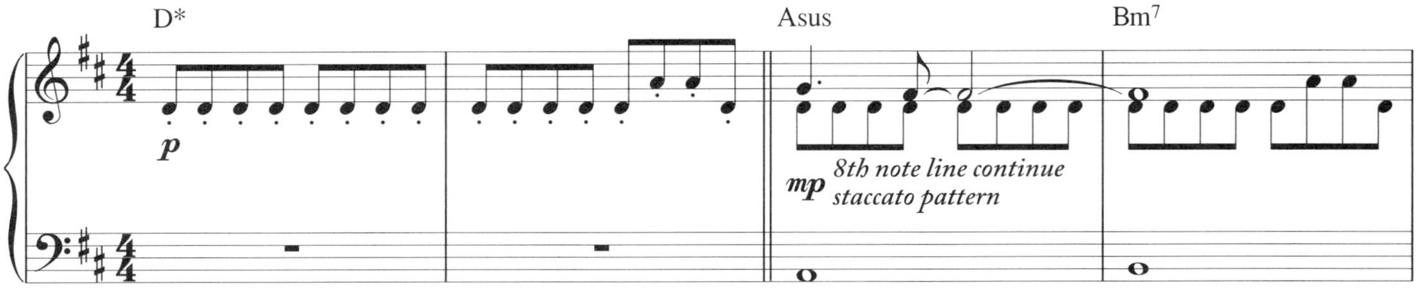

* Chord symbols reflect an overall tonality and do not necessarily indicate specific tonal structures

11
Asus
Bm7
G2(no3)
down. Oh, oh, oh, oh,
14
Asus
Bm7
King of heav-en come down. Oh, oh, oh, oh,
17
G2(no3)
D/F#
Em7
D
Asus
King of heav-en come down. Oh, oh,
20
Bm7
G2(no3)
f
oh, oh.
1., (2.) We'll
(3. We'll)

CHORUS
23
G2(no3)
Asus
D
sing the gos - pel to the poor.
sing the news of all Your grace.
f
26
G2(no3)
Asus
We'll go to com - fort those
We'll help the bro - ken-heart -
29
Bm7
D/F♯
G2(no3)
who mourn. You'll put to-geth -
- ed praise. You'll put Your glo -
32
Asus
D
G2(no3)
- er what's been torn,
- ry on dis - play,

35
Asus
Bm7
King of heav - en.
King of heav - en.
38
D
3rd time to Coda
Bm
Em/G
Em7
mp
L.H. 8vb
VERSE
42
A
F♯/A♯
Bm
mp
Em/G
We come to-geth-er in the wave of God.
45
Em7
A
F♯/A♯
Bm
We stand to-geth-er in Your great com - pas - sion, pour-ing out our

48
Em/G
Em7
A
F♯/A♯
hearts and lives.
Fill us up with an ex - pec - ta - tion.
CHANNEL
51
Bm
mf
Em/G
Em7
Oh, oh, oh, oh,
mf
54
A
F♯/A♯
Bm
King of heav - en come down. Oh, oh,
56
Em/G
Em7
Repeat every time
f
oh, oh.
2. We'll
3. We'll
L.H. as written

CODA
Asus
Bm7
G2(no3)
BRIDGE
You help the bro-ken cit-ies rise;
out of the wreck-age, You bring life.
1.
2.
1. We'll
(2. We'll)

CHORUS
73
G2(no3)
Asus
D
sing the gos - pel to the poor.
sing the news of all Your grace.
f
76
G2(no3)
Asus
We'll go to com - fort those
We'll help the bro - ken-heart -
79
Bm7
D/F♯
G2(no3)
who mourn. You'll put to-geth -
- ed praise. You'll put Your glo -
82
Asus
D
G2(no3)
- er what's been torn,
- ry on dis - play,

Chords Used in This Song

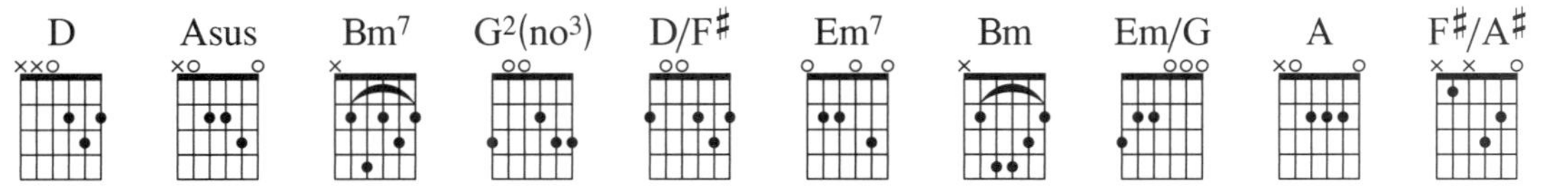

You Alone Can Rescue

Words and Music by
MATT REDMAN
and JONAS MYRIN

Capo 4 (G)

Worshipfully ♩ = 76

7
G♯m7 (Em7) B/D♯ (G/B) E (C) B (G)
shame was deep - er than the sea. Your
9
E (C) F♯sus (Dsus)
1. B (G)
2. B (G)
f
grace is deep - er still.
still. And You a-lone can
CHORUS
12
E (C) F♯sus (Dsus) G♯m7 (Em7)
res - cue, You a - lone can save. You a - lone can
f
14
E (C) F♯sus (Dsus) G♯m7 (Em7)
lift us from the grave. You came down to

16
E (C)
F♯sus (Dsus)
G♯m7 (Em7)
find us, led us out of death. To You a - lone be -
2nd time to Coda
18
E (C)
F♯ (D)
Bsus (Gsus)
B (G)
Bsus (Gsus)
B (G)
longs the high - est praise.
21
mf
VERSE 2
E (C)
B (G)
2. You, O Lord, have made a way. The
mf
23
E (C)
F♯sus (Dsus)
F♯ (D)
great di - vide, You healed. For

25
G♯m7 (Em7) B/D♯ (G/B) E (C) B (G)
when our hearts were far a - way, Your
27
E (C) F♯sus (Dsus) B (G)
love went fur - ther still. Yes, Your
29
E (C) F♯sus (Dsus) B (G)
f
D.S. al Coda
love goes fur - ther still. And You a - lone can
CODA
31
B (G) E (C) F♯sus (Dsus)
And You a - lone can res - cue, You a - lone can

33
G♯m7 (Em7) E (C) F♯sus (Dsus)
save. You a - lone can lift us from __ the grave. __
35
G♯m7 (Em7) E (C) F♯sus (Dsus)
__ You came down to find us, led us out of
37
G♯m7 (Em7) E (C) F♯ (D)
death. To You a - lone be - longs the high - est praise. __
39
G♯m7 (Em7) E (C) F♯ (D) Bsus (Gsus) B (G)
__ To You a - lone be - longs the high - est praise. __

42
Bsus (Gsus)
B (G)
Bsus (Gsus)
B (G)
Bsus (Gsus)
B (G)
ff
We lift _
BRIDGE
45
B (G)
E2(no3) (C2(no3))
_ up our eyes, lift _ up our eyes. You're the giv-er of life. We lift _
ff
47
B (G)
E2(no3) (C2(no3))
_ up our eyes, lift _ up our eyes. You're the giv-er of life. We lift _
49
G♯m7 (Em7)
E2(no3) (C2(no3))
_ up our eyes, lift _ up our eyes. You're the giv-er of life. We lift _

51
G♯m7
(Em7)
1.
E2(no3)
(C2(no3))
up our eyes, lift up our eyes. You're the giv - er of life. We lift
53
2.
E2(no3)
(C2(no3))
giv - er of life.
p
And You a - lone can
CHORUS
E2(no3)
(C2(no3))
F♯sus/A♯
(Dsus/F♯)
res - cue, You a - lone can
p
56
G♯m7
(Em7)
save. You a - lone can
E2(no3)
(C2(no3))
F♯sus/A♯
(Dsus/F♯)
lift us from the grave.
G♯m7
(Em7)
You came down to
59
E2(no3)
(C2(no3))
F♯sus/A♯
(Dsus/F♯)
find us, led us out of
G♯m7
(Em7)
death. To You a - lone be -

Chords Used in This Song

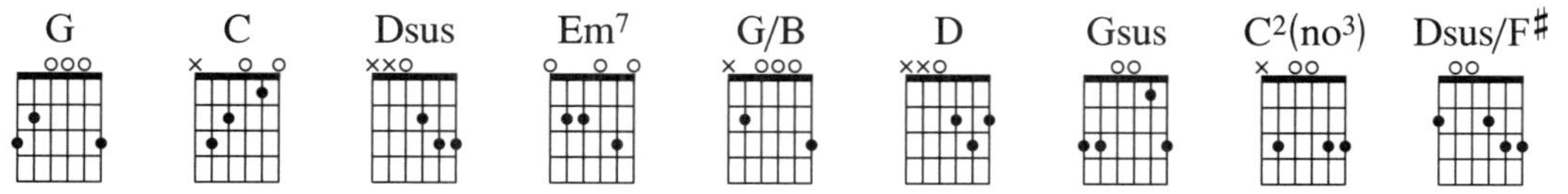

Where the Spirit of the Lord Is

Words and Music by
CHRIS TOMLIN, CHRISTY NOCKELS
and NATHAN NOCKELS

10
E♭m7
(C♯m7)
D♭sus
(Bsus)
Spir - it of the Lord is.
Where the Spir - it of the Lord is, there is lib - er - ty.
C♭2
(A2)
13
E♭m7
(C♯m7)
We're Yours, and Yours is the king - dom,
We are Yours,
D♭sus
(Bsus)
16
C♭2
(A2)
Yours is the king - dom.
Yours is the king - dom.
Oh!
C♭2
(A2)
19
E♭m7
(C♯m7)
f

22
D♭sus (Bsus)
C♭2 (A2)
25
E♭m7 (C♯m7)
D♭sus (Bsus)
VERSE 1
E♭m7 (C♯m7)
mp
1. You are the fire
mp
28
through the night,
A♭m7 (F♯m7)
You are the flame
R.H. sim.
30
that burns inside;
E♭m7 (C♯m7)
we need Your pres-

32
A♭m7
(F♯m7)
-ence more than an-y-thing.
VERSE 2, 3
35
E♭m7
(C♯m7)
2. More than just a song to sing,
3. You call us clos-er to Your heart;
37
A♭m7
(F♯m7)
more than words and of-fer-ings;
lead us, Lord, to where You are.
39
E♭m7
(C♯m7)
we need Your pres-ence more than an-
We need Your pres-ence more than an-

CHANNEL
41
A♭m7
(F♯m7)
mf
C♭2
(A2)
y - thing. And You're all that we want,
y - thing.
mf R.H. end staccato pattern
44
E♭m7
(C♯m7)
D♭sus
(Bsus)
You're all that we need. You're all
47
C♭2
(A2)
E♭m7
(C♯m7)
that we want, You're all that we need.
CHORUS
50
D♭sus
(Bsus)
C♭2
(A2)
f
We know where the Spir - it of the Lord is.
Where the
f

53
E♭m7 (C♯m7)
D♭sus (Bsus)
C♭2 (A2)
Spir - it of the Lord is, there is lib - er - ty.
We know,
56
E♭m7 (C♯m7)
D♭sus (Bsus)
liv - ing in Your free - dom.
Liv - ing in Your free - dom, we see Your glo - ry.
59
C♭2 (A2)
E♭m7 (C♯m7)
We know where the Spir - it of the Lord is.
Where the Spir - it of the Lord is,
62
D♭sus (Bsus)
C♭2 (A2)
We're Yours, and Yours is the king - dom,
there is lib - er - ty.

65
E♭m7
(C♯m7)
D♭sus
(Bsus)
C♭2
(A2)
Yours is the king - dom.
We are Yours, Yours is the king - dom.
ff
68
E♭m7
(C♯m7)
1.
D♭sus
(Bsus)
Yours is the king - dom.
Yours is the king - dom.
71
2.
D♭sus
(Bsus)
C♭2
(A2)
CHANNEL
74
E♭m7
(C♯m7)
D♭sus
(Bsus)
mp
A♭m7
(F♯m7)
And You're all that we want,
mp

77
G♭/B♭
(E/G♯)
You're all that we need. You're all
80
C♭2
(A2)
E♭m7
(C♯m7)
that we want, You're all that we need.
CHORUS
83
D♭sus
(Bsus)
C♭2
(A2)
We know where the Spir - it of the Lord is.
Where the
86
E♭m7
(C♯m7)
D♭sus
(Bsus)
C♭2
(A2)
Spir - it of the Lord is, there is lib - er - ty.
We know,

89
E♭m7
(C♯m7)
D♭sus
(Bsus)
liv - ing in Your free - dom.
Liv - ing in Your free - dom, we see Your glo - ry.
C♭2
(A2)
grad. cresc.
92
E♭m7
(C♯m7)
We know where the Spir - it of the Lord is.
Where the Spir - it of the Lord is,
grad. cresc.
D♭sus
(Bsus)
95
C♭2
(A2)
We're Yours, and Yours is the king - dom,
there is lib - er - ty.
98
E♭m7
(C♯m7)
D♭sus
(Bsus)
Yours is the king - dom.
We are Yours, Yours is the king - dom.

100
C♭2
(A2)
ff
We know where the Spir - it of the Lord is.
Where the
ff
102
E♭m7
(C♯m7)
Spir - it of the Lord is,
D♭sus
(Bsus)
there is lib - er - ty.
104
C♭2
(A2)
We know where the Spir - it of the Lord is.
Where the
106
E♭m7
(C♯m7)
Spir - it of the Lord is,
D♭sus
(Bsus)
there is lib - er - ty.

108
C♭2
(A2)
We know where the Spir - it of the Lord is.
Where the
110
E♭m7
(C♯m7)
D♭sus
(Bsus)
Spir - it of the Lord is, there is lib - er - ty.
112
C♭2
(A2)
We know where the Spir - it of the Lord is.
Where the
114
E♭m7
(C♯m7)
D♭sus
(Bsus)
Spir - it of the Lord is, there is lib - er - ty.

Chords Used in This Song

Rise and Sing

Words and Music by
STEVE FEE

15
B7/D♯
(G7/B)
E
(C)
B7(no3)
(G7(no3))
and sing, rise and sing. If you've been touched by the
18
E
(C)
B7/D♯
(G7/B)
E
(C)
Mer-cy King, rise and sing, rise and sing.
21
ff
B5
(G5)
Woh. Woh.
ff
25
Woh. Woh.

VERSE 2, 3
29
B7/D♯
(G7/B)
E
(C)
2. If you were bound but now you're free, rise
3. If in your heart rings a mel - o - dy, rise
31
and sing, rise and sing.
and sing, rise and sing.
33
Lift up a shout of vic - to - ry, rise
If you have tast - ed and you have seen, rise
35
F♯sus
(Dsus)
B5
(G5)
and sing, rise and sing. Woh.
and sing, rise and sing.

38
Woh.
CHORUS
41
N.C.
B
(G)
B/D♯
(G/B)
Our God is ris - en and reign - ing, and
44
G♯m7
(Em7)
F♯sus
(Dsus)
E2(no3)
(C2(no3))
B
(G)
we're el - e - vat - ing the glo - ry of
47
B/D♯
(G/B)
G♯m7
(Em7)
3rd time to Coda
our God and King.

1.
49
F♯ (D) N.C.
B (G)
B/D♯ (G/B)
Ev - 'ry - bod - y rise and sing.
52
G♯m7 (Em7)
F♯7 (D7)
Emaj7 (Cmaj7)
B (G)
B/D♯ (G/B)
56
G♯m7 (Em7)
F♯7 (D7)
Emaj7 (Cmaj7)
2.
F♯sus (Dsus)
E2(no3) (C2(no3))
D.S. al Coda
'Cause our God is
CODA
59
F♯ (D) N.C.
B (G)
B/D♯ (G/B)
Ev - 'ry - bod - y rise and sing.

62
G♯m7 (Em7)
F♯7 (D7)
Emaj7 (Cmaj7)
B5 (G5)
66
BRIDGE
f
Let the re-deemed of the
69
Lord _ sing, "Hal-le - lu - jah!" (Hal-le - lu - jah!)
F♯ (D)
E2 (C2)
72
B5 (G5)
Let the re-deemed of the Lord _ sing, "Our God reigns!" (Our God

75
F♯sus (Dsus) F♯ (D) E2 (C2) B5 (G5) B/D♯ (G/B)
reigns!) Let the re-deemed of the Lord sing, "Hal-le-lu-
78
G♯m7 (Em7) F♯sus (Dsus) E2 (C2) B5 (G5)
-jah!" (Hal-le-lu-jah!) Let the re-deemed of the
81
Bmaj7/D♯ (Gmaj7/B) G♯m7 (Em7) F♯sus (Dsus) E2 (C2)
Lord sing, "Our God reigns!" (Our God reigns!)
84
B5 (G5) B/D♯ (G/B) G♯m7 (Em7)
Let the re-deemed of the Lord sing, "Hal-le-lu-jah!" (Hal-le-lu-

87
F♯sus (Dsus) E2 (C2) B5 (G5) Bmaj7/D♯ (Gmaj7/B)
- jah!) Let the re deemed of the Lord sing, "Our God
90
G♯m7 (Em7) F♯sus (Dsus) N.C. F♯sus (Dsus) N.C.
ff
reigns!" (Our God reigns!) Our God is
CHORUS
B (G)
ris - en and
ff
94
B/D♯ (G/B) G♯m7 (Em7) F♯sus (Dsus) E2(no3) (C2(no3))
reign - ing, and we're el - e - vat - ing the
97
B (G) B/D♯ (G/B) G♯m7 (Em7)
glo - ry of our God and King.

F♯sus (Dsus) E2(no3) (C2(no3)) B (G) N.C. B/D♯ (G/B)
100
'Cause our God is ris - en and reign - ing, and
G♯m (Em) N.C. E (C) B (G) N.C.
103
we're el - e - vat - ing the glo - ry of
B/D♯ (G/B) G♯m (Em) N.C.
106
our God and King. 'Cause our God is
B (G) B/D♯ (G/B) G♯m7 (Em7)
109
ris - en and reign - ing, and we're el - e -

Chords Used in This Song

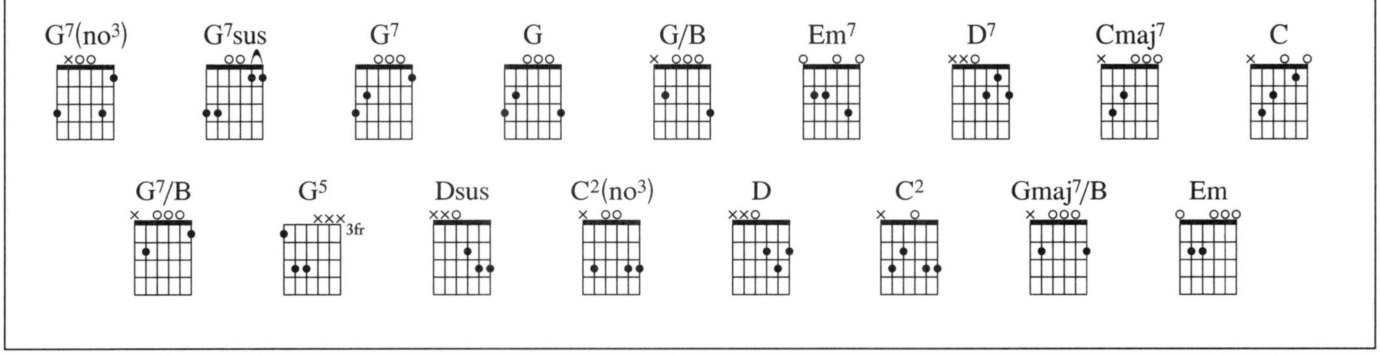

Like a Lion

Words and Music by
DANIEL BASHTA

Capo 4 (Em) With passion ♩ = 128

VERSE
17
3.
G♯m7
(Em7)
mf
F♯sus
(Dsus)
1., 2. Let love ex - plode, and bring the
3., 4. Let hope a - rise, and make the
mp
20
B
(G)
C♯m7
(Am7)
dead to life; a love so
dark - ness hide. My faith is
23
B
(G)
E
(C)
1., 3.
bold to see a rev - o - lu - tion some - how.
dead; I need a res - ur - rec - tion some - how.
CHANNEL
26
2., 4.
F♯(add4)
(D(add4))
some - how. Now I'm lost in Your free -
some - how.
mf

29
G♯m7
(Em7)
F♯(add4)
(D(add4))
- dom; oh, this
32
E
(C)
f
world I'll o - ver - come. My God's
CHORUS
35
F♯
(D)
N.C.
G♯m7
(Em7)
not dead, He's sure - ly a - live; and He's liv - ing on the in - side,
f
38
F♯(add4)
(D(add4))
roar - ing like a lion. My God's not dead, He's

40
G♯m7
(Em7)
2nd time to Coda
sure-ly a-live; and He's liv-ing on the in-side,
42
F♯
(D)
roar-ing like a lion.
45
B
(G)
G♯m7
(Em7)
48
F♯
(D)
B
(G)
D.S. al Coda

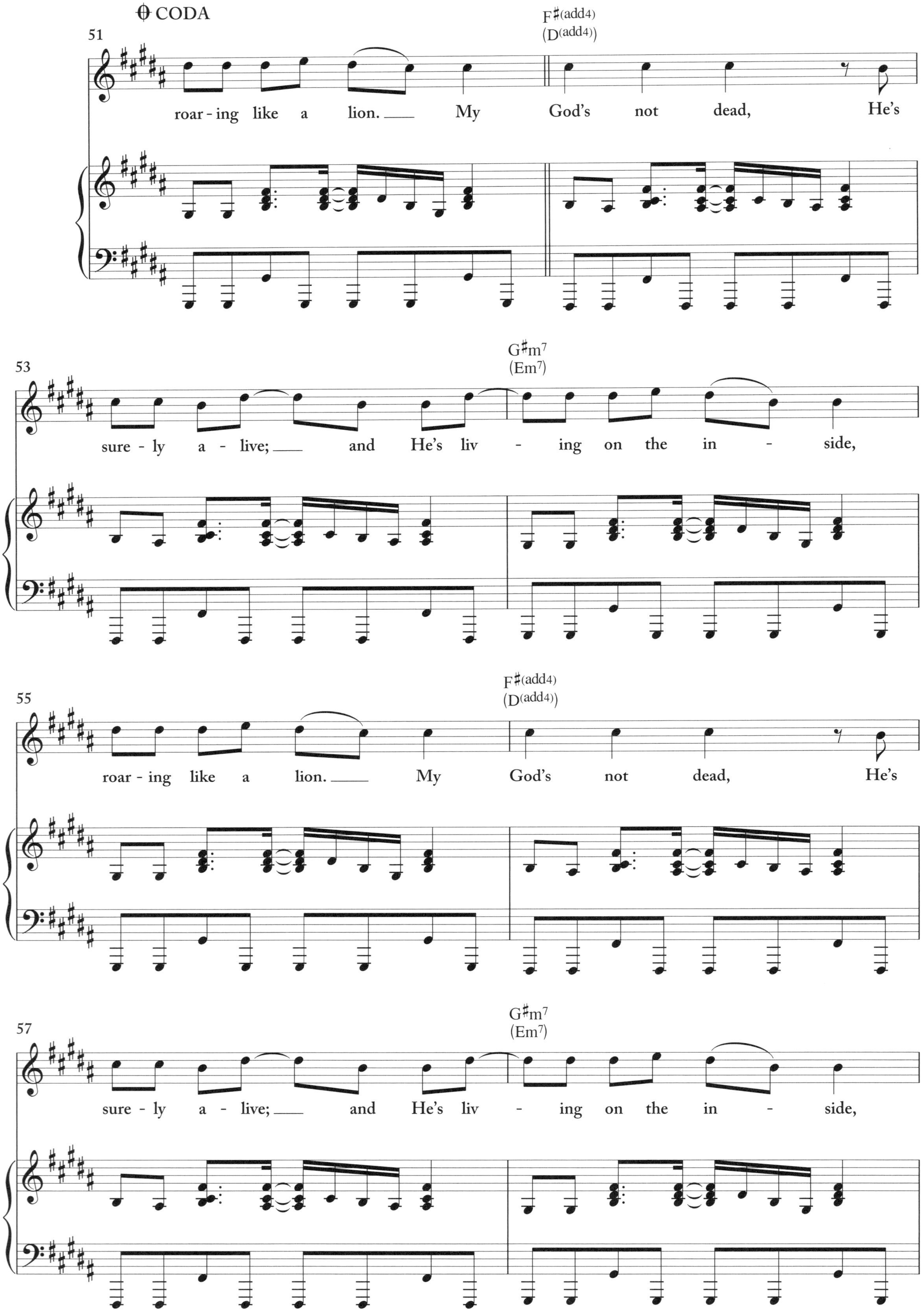
CODA
51
F♯(add4)
(D(add4))
roar - ing like a lion. My God's not dead, He's
53
G♯m7
(Em7)
sure - ly a - live; and He's liv - ing on the in - side,
55
F♯(add4)
(D(add4))
roar - ing like a lion. My God's not dead, He's
57
G♯m7
(Em7)
sure - ly a - live; and He's liv - ing on the in - side,

59
B2
(G2)
roar-ing like a lion.
62
F#sus/A#
(Dsus/F#)
G#m7
(Em7)
He's sure-ly a-live!
Oh, He's
65
E
(C)
mp
sure-ly a-live!
Let heav - en
BRIDGE
68
B2
(G2)
build 3rd time
F#sus/A#
(Dsus/F#)
roar
and fire
fall;
mp
build 3rd time

71
G♯m7
(Em7)
3
come shake the ground with the sound of re -
74
C♯m7
(Am7)
1., 2.
3.
f
vi - val. Let heav - en
Let heav - en
77
B2
(G2)
F♯sus/A♯
(Dsus/F♯)
f
roar and fire fall;
80
G♯m7
(Em7)
come shake the ground with the sound of re -

83
C♯m7
(Am7)
1.
2.
ff
vi - val!
Let heav - en
My God's
86
F♯
(D)
N.C.
not dead, He's sure - ly a - live; and He's liv -
ff
88
G♯m7
(Em7)
- ing on the in - side, roar - ing like a lion. My
90
F♯(add4)
(D(add4))
God's not dead, He's sure - ly a - live; and He's liv -

92
G♯m7
(Em7)
- ing on the in - side, roar - ing like a lion. My
94
F♯(add4)
(D(add4))
God's not dead, He's sure - ly a - live; and He's liv -
96
G♯m7
(Em7)
- ing on the in - side, roar - ing like a lion. My
98
F♯(add4)
(D(add4))
God's not dead, He's sure - ly a - live; and He's liv -

100
G♯m7
(Em7)
- ing on the in - side, roar - ing like a lion.
102
F♯
(D)
B
(G)
Oh, He's sure - ly a - live!
105
G♯m7
(Em7)
Oh, He's sure - ly a - live!
107
F♯
(D)
B
(G)
Oh, He's sure - ly a - live!

Chords Used in This Song

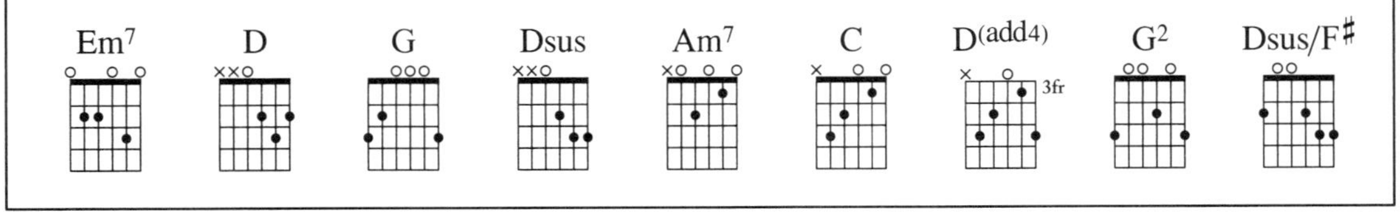

Chosen Generation

Words and Music by
CHRIS TOMLIN, LOUIE GIGLIO,
DANIEL CARSON, and JESSE REEVES

Capo 4 (G)

With energy! ♩ = 139

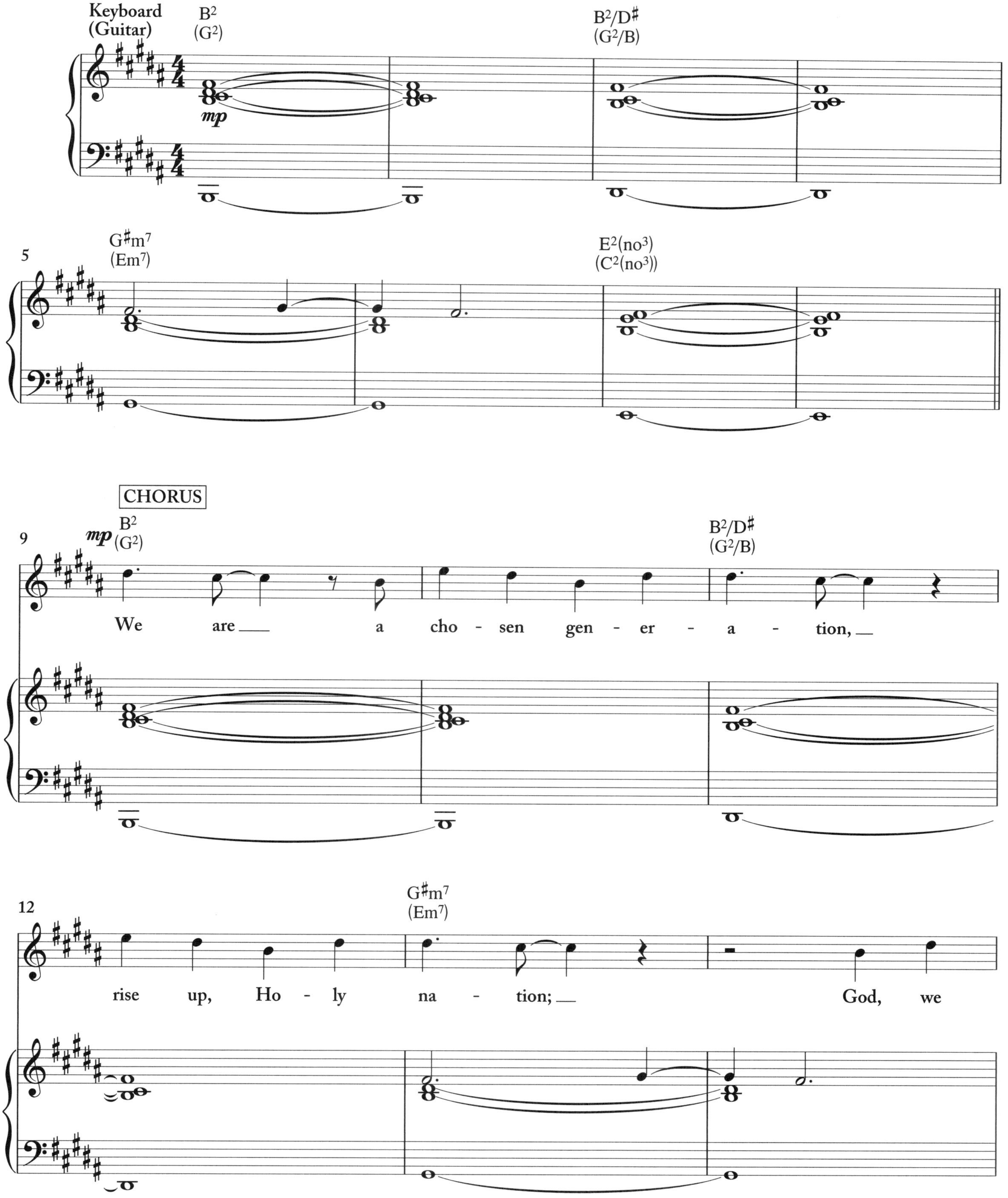

15
E2(no3)
(C2(no3))
B2
(G2)
live for You.
You have
18
B2/D♯
(G2/B)
called us out of dark - ness
in - to light so
21
G♯m7
(Em7)
E2(no3)
(C2(no3))
building in intensity
glo - ri - ous;
God, we live for You,
building in intensity
24
we live for You,
God, we

27
live for You.
VERSE
30
mp
E2(no3)
(C2(no3))
We run with pas - sion for Your name, we
mp
33
B2/D♯
(G2/B)
B2
(G2)
E2(no3)
(C2(no3))
run.
Free - dom, You've bro -
36
B2/D♯
(G2/B)
B2
(G2)
- ken ev - 'ry chain, we run.

39
E2(no3)
(C2(no3))
B2
(G2)
And our God will not be moved; our God will
42
C♯7(add4)
(A7(add4))
mf
nev - er be sha - ken. We run to You, we
mf
45
E2(no3)
(C2(no3))
CHORUS
f
B2
(G2)
run! We are a
f
48
B2/D♯
(G2/B)
cho - sen gen - er - a - tion, rise up, Ho - ly

51
G♯m7
(Em7)
E2(no3)
(C2(no3))
na - tion; God, we live for You.
54
B2
(G2)
You have called us out of
57
B2/D♯
(G2/B)
G♯m7
(Em7)
dark - ness in - to light so glo - ri - ous;
60
E2(no3)
(C2(no3))
2nd time to Coda
God, we live for You.

D.S. al Coda
63
CODA
67
E2(no3)
(C2(no3))
N.C.
And our God will not be moved; our God will
drums continue
70
nev - er be sha - ken. our God will not be moved;
73
our God will nev - er be sha - ken.
E2(no3)
(C2(no3))
And our God will

76
B2/D♯
(G2/B)
B2
(G2)
not be moved; our God will nev - er be sha - ken.
79
C♯7(add4)
(A7(add4))
E2(no3)
(C2(no3))
We run to You, we run!
CHORUS
82
B2
(G2)
We are a cho - sen gen - er -
85
B2/D♯
(G2/B)
G♯m7
(Em7)
a - tion, rise up, Ho - ly na - tion;

88
E2(no3)
(C2(no3))
God, we live for You.
91
B2
(G2)
B2/D♯
(G2/B)
You have called us out of dark - ness
94
G♯m7
(Em7)
in - to light so glo - ri - ous;
96
E2(no3)
(C2(no3))
ff
God, we live for You.
You are

BRIDGE
99
B2 (G2)
E2(no3) (C2(no3))
ev - 'ry - thing, more than all we need;
world to be not e - nough for me.
ff
102
B2/D♯ (G2/B)
God, we live for You, God, we
God, we live for You, God, we
105
C♯m7(4) (Am7(4))
1.
2.
live for You. I found this
live for You.
108
B2 (G2)
E2(no3) (C2(no3))

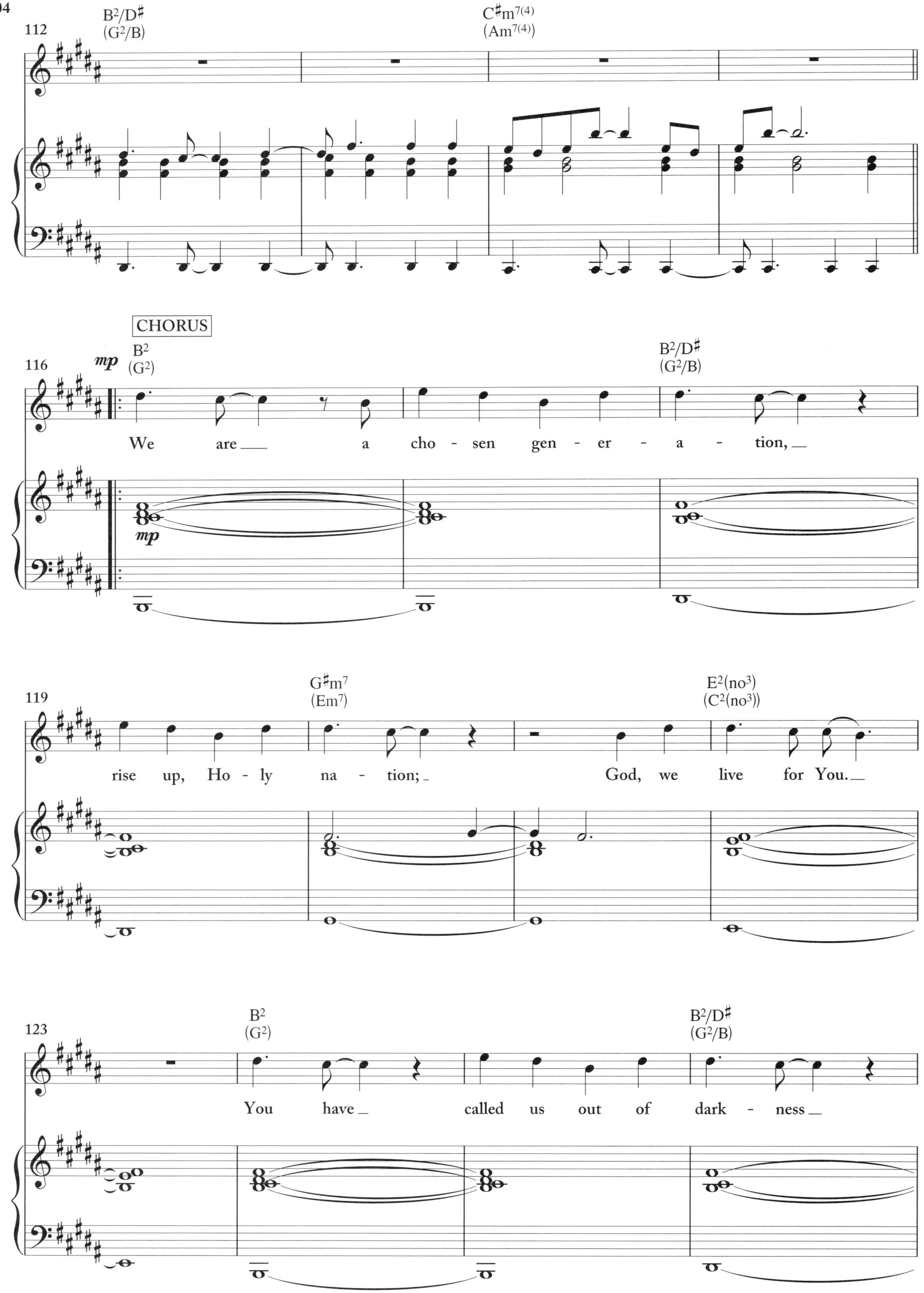
112
B2/D♯
(G2/B)
C♯m7(4)
(Am7(4))
CHORUS
116
mp
B2
(G2)
B2/D♯
(G2/B)
We are a cho - sen gen - er - a - tion,
mp
119
G♯m7
(Em7)
E2(no3)
(C2(no3))
rise up, Ho - ly na - tion;
God, we live for You.
123
B2
(G2)
B2/D♯
(G2/B)
You have called us out of dark - ness

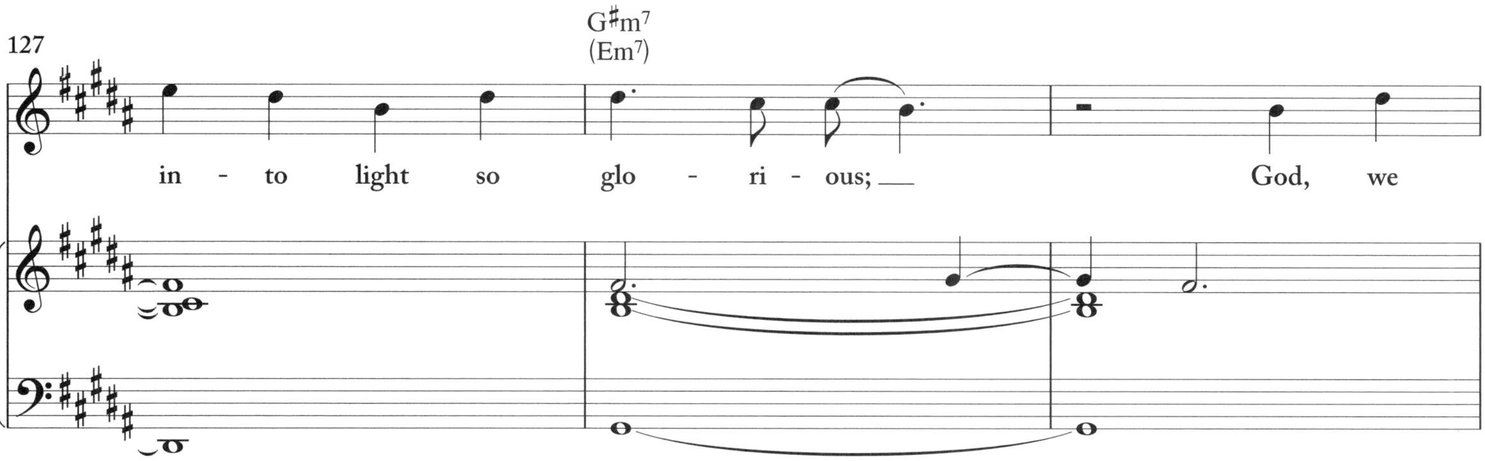

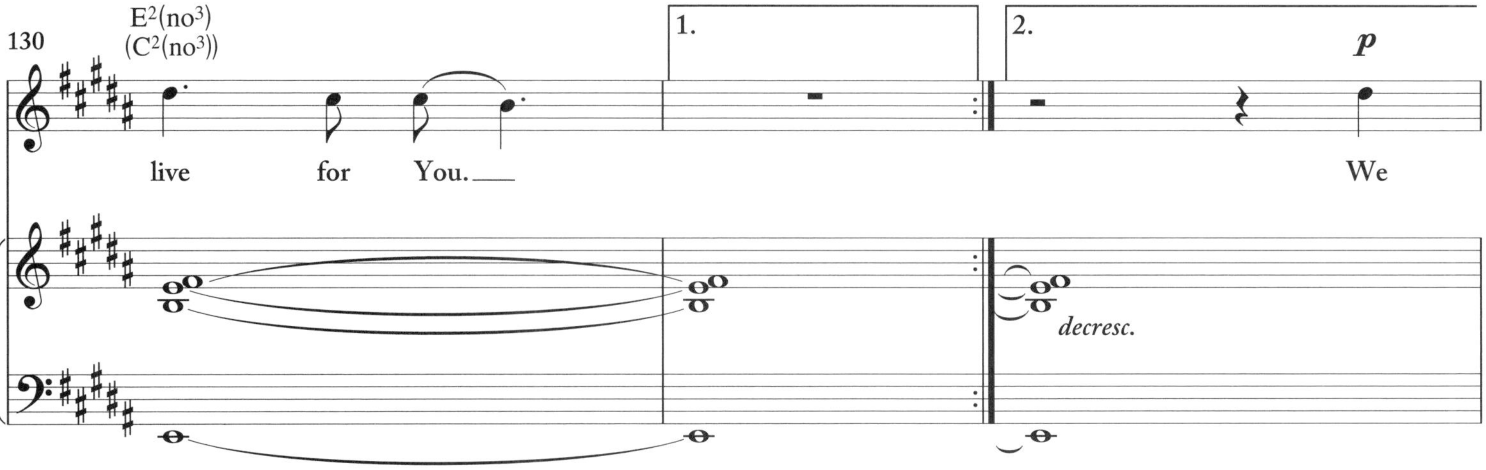

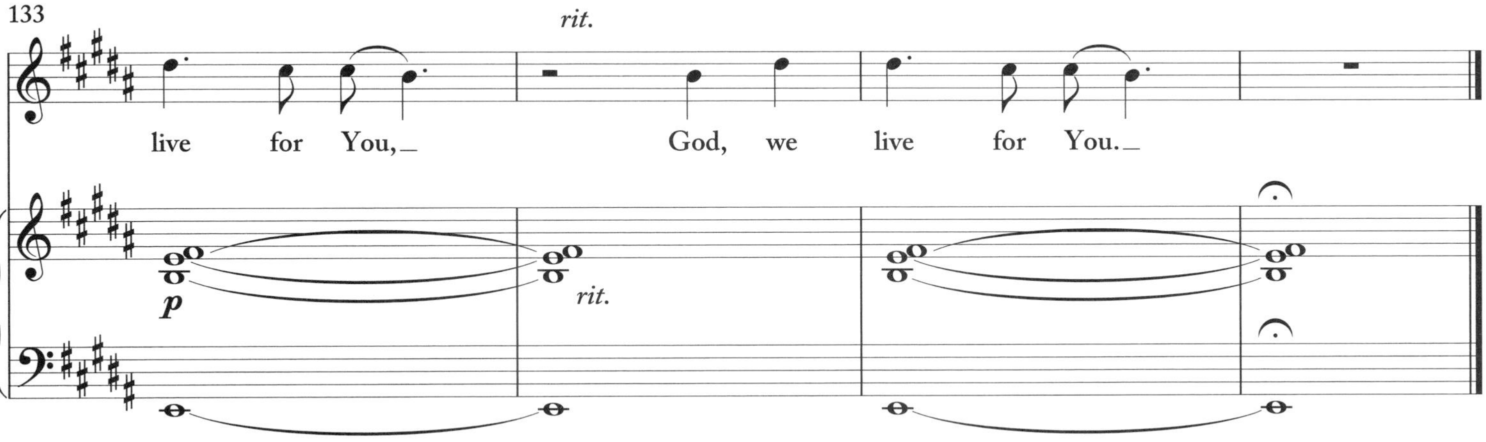

Chords Used in This Song

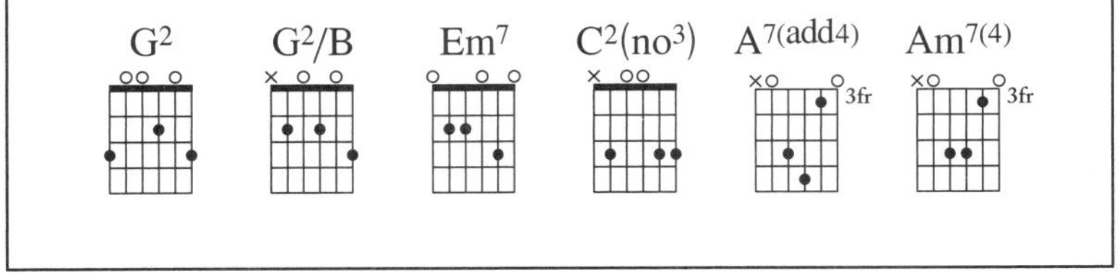

With Everything

Capo 4 (G)

Words and Music by
JOEL HOUSTON

8
B2 (G2)
F♯(add4) (D(add4))
a beau - ti - ful God.
CHANNEL
10
E2 (C2)
mp
G♯m7 (Em7)
And there is no oth - er name like Je -
12
B2 (G2)
F♯(add4) (D(add4))
E2 (C2)
- sus. We give You all of the praise,
15
G♯m7 (Em7)
B2 (G2)
F♯(add4) (D(add4))
mf
O Lord, Je - sus. So let hope

CHORUS
G♯m7 (Em7) E (C) B (G) F♯(add4) (D(add4))
rise, and dark-ness trem-ble in Your
ho-ly light that ev-'ry eye will see
Je-sus, our God, great and might-y to
be praised. So let hope
mf

26
G♯m7 (Em7) cresc. E (C) B (G) F♯(add4) (D(add4))
— rise, and dark - ness trem - ble — in Your
cresc.
28
G♯m7 (Em7) E (C) B (G) F♯(add4) (D(add4))
ho - ly light — that ev - 'ry eye will see
30
E2 (C2) f G♯m7 (Em7) F♯(add4) (D(add4)) C♯m7 (Am7)
Je - sus, our — God, great and might - y — to —
f
32
E2 (C2) F♯(add4) (D(add4))
— be praised. —

BRIDGE

34
ff
B2 (G2)
F♯(add4) (D(add4))
God of all days, glo - ri - ous in
ff
36
G♯m7 (Em7)
E2 (C2)
all of Your ways; the maj - es - ty, the
38
B2 (G2)
F♯(add4) (D(add4))
won - der, and grace in the light of Your
40
G♯m7 (Em7)
E2 (C2)
f
name. So let hope

CHORUS
G♯m7 (Em7) E2 (C2) B (G) F♯(add4) (D(add4))
rise, and dark-ness trem - ble in Your
G♯m7 (Em7) E2 (C2) B (G) F♯(add4) (D(add4))
ho - ly light that ev-'ry eye will see
E2 (C2) G♯m7 (Em7) F♯(add4) (D(add4)) C♯m7 (Am7)
Je - sus, our God, great and might - y to
E2 (C2) F♯(add4) (D(add4)) E (C)
be praised.
f
sub. p

51
G♯m7 (Em7)
B (G)
F♯(add4) (D(add4))
mp
With ev -
BREAKDOWN
54
E (C)
building 2nd time
G♯m7 (Em7)
- 'ry - thing, with ev - 'ry - thing, we will
mp
L.H. play 8th notes 2nd time, as cued
building 2nd time
56
B (G)
F♯(add4) (D(add4))
shout for Your glo - ry. With ev -
58
E (C)
G♯m7 (Em7)
- 'ry - thing, with ev - 'ry - thing, we will

60
B
(G)
1.
F♯(add4)
(D(add4))
2.
F♯(add4)
(D(add4))
ff
shout forth Your praise. With ev - praise. Our hearts,
63
E2
(C2)
G♯m7
(Em7)
they cry, "Be glo - ri - fied! Be lift -
ff
65
B2
(G2)
F♯(add4)
(D(add4))
- ed high a - bove all!" For You,
67
E2
(C2)
G♯m7
(Em7)
our King, with ev - 'ry - thing, we will

Chords Used in This Song

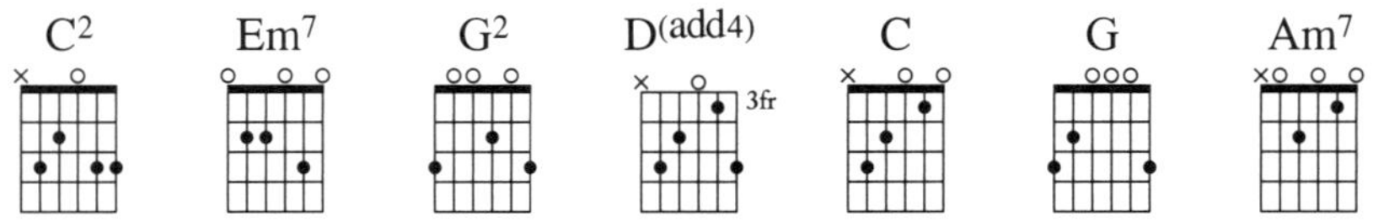

Awakening

CHRIS TOMLIN and REUBEN MORGAN

KEY OF (E♭)

Dmaj7 A(add4) G G2(no3) Bm7 D2(no3) A Em7 D

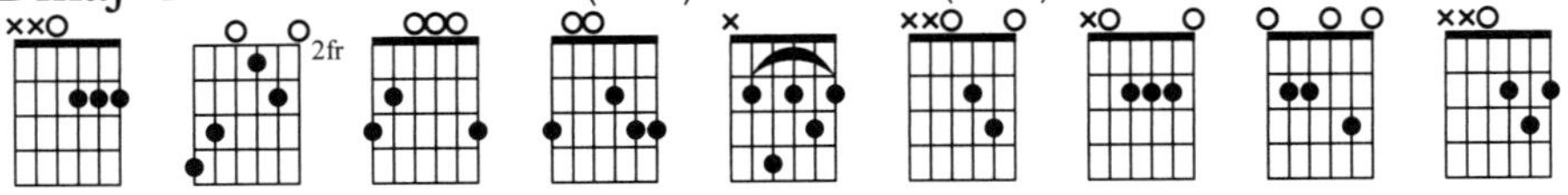

capo 1st fret (D)

Dmaj7

VERSE 1:

Dmaj7 A(add4)
In our hearts, Lord, in this nation
G Dmaj7
Awakening.
A(add4) G Dmaj7
Holy Spirit, we de - sire awakening.

CHORUS:

G2(no3) Bm7
For You, and You alone awake my soul;
D2(no3) A
Awake my soul, and sing.
G2(no3) Bm7
For the world You love Your will be done,
D2(no3) A
Let Your will be done in me.

VERSE 2:

Dmaj7 A(add4)
In Your presence, in Your power,
G Dmaj7
Awakening.
A(add4) G Dmaj7
For this moment, in this hour, awakening.

(repeat CHORUS 2x)

G Em7 Bm7 D2(no3)

Em7 G A

BRIDGE:

G Em7
Like the rising sun that shines,
Bm7 D2(no3)
From the darkness comes a light;
Em7 G
I hear Your voice, and this is my
Em7 A
Awakening! ***(repeat)***

G Bm7 D A G Bm7 D A

G
Like the rising sun that shines,
Bm7 D
Awake my soul, awake my soul and sing.
A G
From the darkness comes a light;
Bm7 D
Awake my soul, awake my soul and sing.
G
Like the rising sun that shines,
Bm7 D
Awake my soul, awake my soul and sing.
A G
Only You can raise a life;
Bm7 D
Awake my soul, awake my soul and sing.

Dmaj7 A(add4)
In our hearts, Lord, in the nations—
G Dmaj7
Awakening.

Say Say

KRISTIAN STANFILL, CHRIS TOMLIN, and CHRISTY NOCKELS

KEY OF (C)

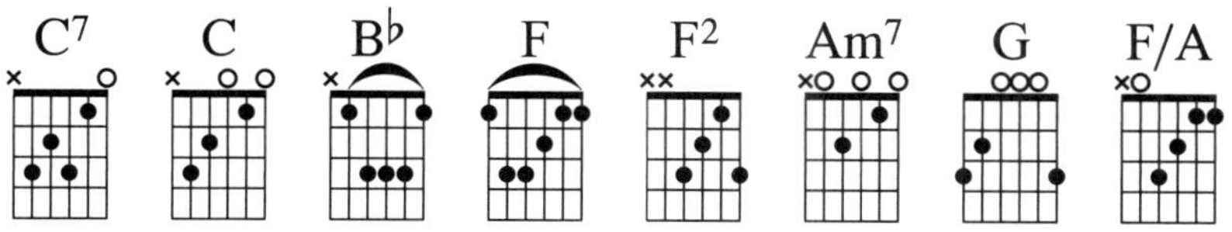

C7

VERSE 1:

C
Some hope in what their eyes can see;
B♭
We hope in the glorious unseen,
F
In a risen and returning King.
C
Some are chasing the treasures of this world;
B♭
we run to a glorious reward,
F
The only name worth living for!   Say, say!

CHORUS:

C
Say, say, say you believe it;
F2
Sing for the whole world to hear it.
Am7   F2   G
We know, and we declare it: "Jesus is King!"
C
Say, say, say you believe it;
F2
Sing loud, sing like you mean it.
Am7   F2   G
We know, and we declare it: "Jesus is King!"

Say, say!

C7

VERSE 2:

C
We set our hearts on what will last:
B♭
Your Word, Your love, Your faithfulness—
F
Our hope is built on nothing less.
C
We open wide our mouths to praise.
B♭
Let this generation raise
F
A song of freedom all our days!   Say, say!

(repeat CHORUS)

C   B♭

BRIDGE:

C   B♭
I believe Your kingdom come;
    C   B♭
The Son of God, the King of love!
C   B♭
I believe Your kingdom come;
    F/A   B♭
The Son of God, the King of love!

(repeat CHORUS)

C7

C

Our God

MATT REDMAN, JONAS MYRIN, CHRIS TOMLIN, and JESSE REEVES

KEY OF (G♯m)

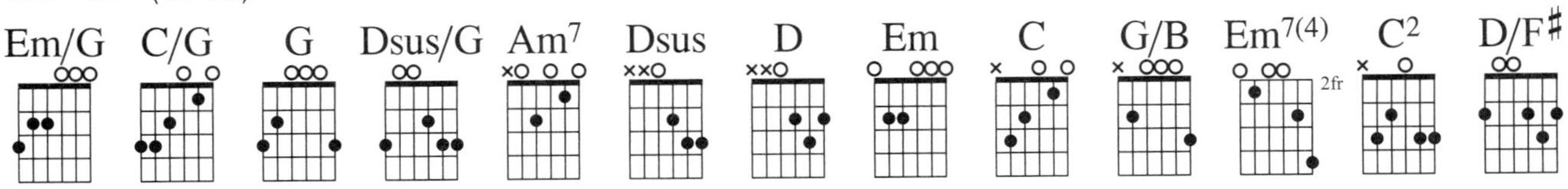

Capo 4th fret (Em)

Em/G C/G G Dsus/G

Em/G C/G G Dsus/G

VERSE 1:

Em/G C/G G
Water You turned into wine,
Em/G C/G G
Opened the eyes of the blind;
Am^{7} Dsus D
There's no one like You, none like You.

VERSE 2:

Em C G
Into the dark - ness, You shine;
Em C G
Out of the ash - es, we rise.
Am^{7} Dsus D
There's no one like You, none like You.

CHORUS:

Em C
Our God is greater, our God is stronger;
G Dsus
God, You are higher than an - y other.
Em C
Our God is healer, awesome in power,
G Dsus
Our God, our God.

Em C G Dsus

(repeat VERSE 2, repeat CHORUS 2x)

Em C G Dsus

Em C G Dsus

BRIDGE:

Em
And if our God is for us
C
Then who could ever stop us,
G
And if our God is with us
Dsus
Then what could stand against?

(repeat)

Em C G/B Dsus

CHORUS 2:

Em$^{7(4)}$ C^{2}
Our God is greater, our God is stronger;
G D/F♯
God, You are higher than an - y other.
Em$^{7(4)}$ C^{2}
Our God is healer, awesome in power,
G D/F♯
Our God, our God.

(repeat)

BRIDGE:

Em$^{7(4)}$
And if our God is for us
C^{2}
Then who could ever stop us,
G
And if our God is with us
D/F♯
Then what could stand against?

(repeat)

Em C G/B Dsus

(repeat CHORUS 2 2x)

How He Loves

JOHN MARK McMILLAN

KEY OF (C)

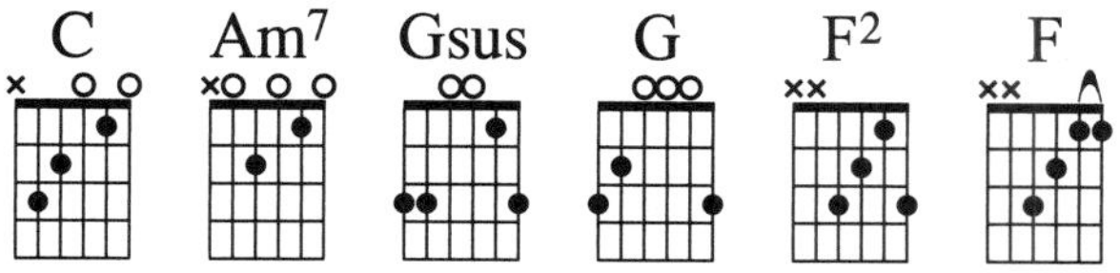

C   Am7   Gsus   G   F2

VERSE 1:

C
He is jealous for me.
Am7
Love's like a hurricane, I am a tree
Gsus   G   F2
Bending beneath the weight of His wind and mercy.
   C
And all of the sudden
                      Am7
I am unaware of these af - flictions eclipsed by glory;
    Gsus   G
And I realize just how beautiful You are,
       F2
And how great Your affections are for me.

CHORUS 1:

C   Am7
Oh, how He loves us, oh,
         Gsus   G   F2
Oh, how He loves us; how He loves us   all.

(repeat VERSE 1 and CHORUS 1)

C   Am7   Gsus   G   F   F2

CHORUS 2:

      C   Am7
Yeah, He loves us, O how He loves us,
        Gsus   G   F   F2
O how He loves us, O how He loves!

VERSE 2:

   C
And we are His portion, and He is our prize,
Am7
Drawn to redemption by the grace in His eyes.
   Gsus   G   F   F2
If His grace is an ocean, we're all sinking.
   C
And heaven meets earth like an unforseen kiss,
       Am7
And my heart turns violently inside of my chest;
  Gsus   G
I don't have time to main - tain these regrets
      F   F2
When I think about the way

(repeat CHORUS 2 2x)

C   Am7
  Oh, He loves us all!
                    Gsus
Oh, how He loves us all!
                  G
Oh, how He loves us all!
        F   F2
Oh, how He loves us all!
      C   Am7
Yeah, He loves us, O how He loves us,
        Gsus   G   F   F2
O how He loves us, O how He loves!
C   Am7   Gsus   G   F   F2

      C   Am7
Yeah, He loves us, O how He loves us,
        Gsus   G   F   F2
O how He loves us, O how He loves!
C

Healing Is in Your Hands

DANIEL CARSON, CHRISTY NOCKELS, NATHAN NOCKELS, MATT REDMAN, and CHRIS TOMLIN

KEY OF (D)

D D/C# Bm7 A Em7 F#m G2(no3) D/F#

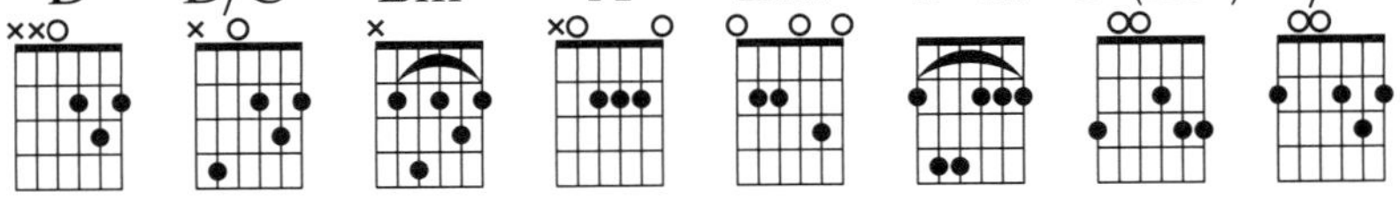

VERSE 1:

D D/C#
No mountain, no valley,
Bm7 A
No gain or loss we know,
Em7 A
Could keep us from Your love.

VERSE 2:

D D/C#
No sickness, no secret,
Bm7 A
No chain is strong enough
Em7 A
Could keep us from Your love,
Em7 A
Could keep us from Your love.

CHORUS:

D A Bm7 F#m
How high how wide;
G2(no3) D/F#
No matter where I am,
F#m G2(no3)
Healing is in Your hands.
D A Bm7 F#m
How deep how strong;
G2(no3) D/F#
Now by Your grace I stand.
F#m G2(no3)
Healing is in Your hands.

VERSE 3:

D D/C#
Our present, our future,
Bm7 A
Our past is in Your hands;

CONTINUED...

Em7 A
We're covered by Your blood,
Em7 A
We're covered by Your blood.

(repeat CHORUS)

BRIDGE:

D D/C#
In all things, we know that
Bm7 A
We are more than conquerors;
Em7 A
You keep us by Your love.
D D/C#
In all things, we know that
Bm7 A
We are more than conquerors;
Em7 A
You keep us by Your love.
Em7 A
You keep us by Your love.

(repeat CHORUS)

King of Heaven (Isaiah 61)

CHARLIE HALL, KENDALL COMBES, BRIAN BERGMAN, DUSTIN RAGLAND, and QUINT ANDERSON

KEY OF (D)

D   Asus   Bm^7 G^2(no^3)   D/F♯   Em^7 Bm   Em/G   A   F♯/A♯

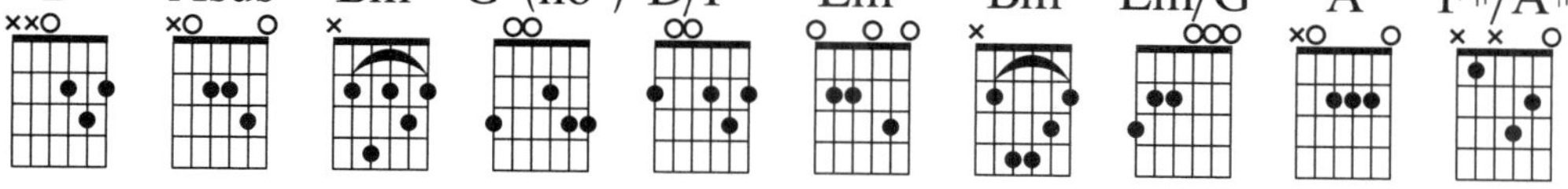

D   Asus   Bm^7 G^2(no^3)

INTRO:

Asus   Bm^7 G^2(no^3)
Oh, oh,   oh, oh,
D/F♯   Em^7 D   Asus
King of heaven come down.
Bm^7 G^2(no^3)
Oh, oh,   oh, oh,
Asus
King of heaven come down.
Asus   Bm^7 G^2(no^3)
Oh, oh,   oh, oh,
D/F♯   Em^7 D   Asus
King of heaven come down.
Bm^7 G^2(no^3)
Oh, oh,   oh, oh.

CHORUS 1:

G^2(no^3)   Asus   D   G^2(no^3)
We'll sing the gos - pel to the poor.
Asus   Bm^7 D/F♯
We'll go to com - fort those who mourn.
G^2(no^3)   Asus   D   G^2(no^3)
You'll put togeth - er what's been torn,
Asus   Bm^7
King of heaven.
D   Bm   Em/G   Em^7 A   F♯/A♯

VERSE:

Bm   Em/G
We come together in the wave of God.
Em^7 A   F♯/A♯
We stand together in Your great com - pas - sion,
Bm   Em/G
Pouring out our hearts and lives.
Em^7 A   F♯/A♯
Fill us up with an expec - ta - tion.

CHANNEL:

Asus   Bm^7 G^2(no^3)
Oh, oh,   oh, oh,
D/F♯   Em^7 D   Asus
King of heaven come down.
Bm^7 G^2(no^3)
Oh, oh,   oh, oh.

(repeat CHORUS 1, VERSE, and CHANNEL)

CHORUS 2:

G^2(no^3)   Asus   D   G^2(no^3)
We'll sing the news of all Your grace.
Asus   Bm^7 D/F♯
We'll help the bro - ken-heart - ed praise.
G^2(no^3)   Asus   D   G^2(no^3)
You'll put Your glo - ry on display,
Asus   Bm^7
King of heaven.
Asus   Bm^7 G^2(no^3)

BRIDGE:

Asus   Bm^7 G^2(no^3)
You help the broken cities rise;
Asus   Bm^7 G^2(no^3)
Out of the wreckage, You bring life.

(repeat)

(repeat CHORUS 1 and CHORUS 2)

G^2(no^3)   Asus
Oh, King of heaven!
N.C. D/F♯   N.C. D

G^2(no^3)

You Alone Can Rescue

MATT REDMAN and JONAS MYRIN

KEY OF (B)

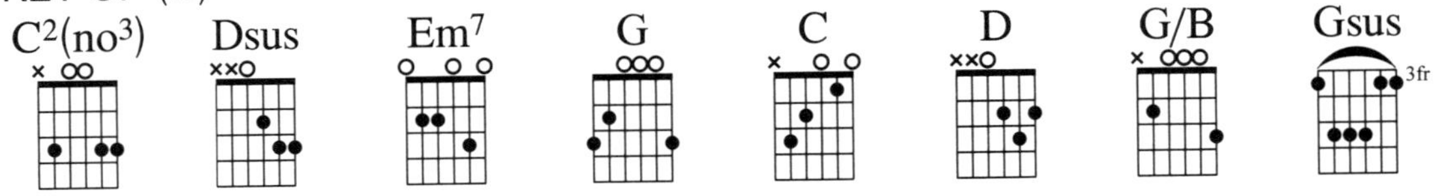

INTRO:
Capo 4 (G)

$C^2(no^3)$ Dsus Em^7 $C^2(no^3)$ Dsus

VERSE 1:
GG C G
Who, O Lord, could save them - selves,
C Dsus E
Their own soul could heal?
Em^7 G/B C G
Our shame was deeper than the sea.
C Dsus G
Your grace is deeper still.

(REPEAT VERSE 1)

CHORUS:
C Dsus Em^7
And You alone can rescue, You alone can save.
C Dsus Em^7
You alone can lift us from the grave.
C Dsus Em^7
You came down to find us, led us out of death.
C E
To You alone be-longs the high - est praise.
1st time only: Gsus G

VERSE 2:
C G
You, O Lord, have made a way.
C Dsus E
The great divide, You healed.
Em^7 G/B C G
For when our hearts were far a-way,
C Dsus G
Your love went further still.
C Dsus G
Yes, Your love goes further still.

(REPEAT CHORUS)

CONTINUED...

Em^7 G C E
To You alone be-longs the hig - hest praise.
G Gsus G Gsus G Gsus G Gsus
You alone.

BRIDGE:
G
We lift up our eyes, lift up our eyes.
$C^2(no^3)$
You're the giver of life.
G
We lift up our eyes, lift up our eyes.
$C^2(no^3)$
You're the giver of life.
Em^7
We lift up our eyes, lift up our eyes.
$C^2(no^3)$
You're the giver of life.
Em^7
We lift up our eyes, lift up our eyes.
$C^2(no^3)$
You're the giver of life.

(REPEAT BRIDGE)

(REPEAT CHORUS)

TAG:
Em^7 C Dsus Em^7
To You alone be-longs the high - est praise.
C Dsus
To You alone be-longs the high - est praise.
$C^2(no^3)$ G/B $C^2(no^3)$ G/B

$C^2(no^3)$ G/B $C^2(no^3)$ G/B G
To You a-lone.

Where the Spirit of the Lord Is

CHRIS TOMLIN, CHRISTY NOCKELS, and NATHAN NOCKELS

KEY OF (E♭m)

A2 C#m7 Bsus F#m7 E/G#

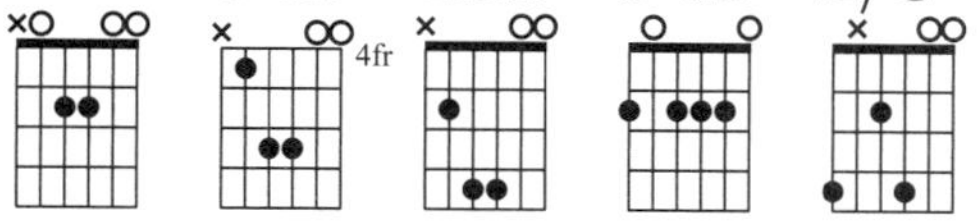

Capo 2nd fret (C#m)

CHORUS:

A2
We know where the Spirit of the Lord is.
C#m7 Bsus
Where the Spirit of the Lord is, there is liberty.
A2
We know, living in Your freedom.
C#m7 Bsus
Living in Your freedom, we see Your glory.
A2
We know where the Spirit of the Lord is.
C#m7 Bsus
Where the Spirit of the Lord is, there is liberty.
A2
We're Yours, and Yours is the kingdom,
C#m7 Bsus A2
We are Yours, Yours is the kingdom.

A2 C#m7 Bsus A2 C#m7 Bsus

VERSE 1, 2:

C#m7 F#m7
You are the fire through the night,
C#m7
You are the flame that burns inside;
F#m7
We need Your presence more than an - ything.
C#m7 F#m7
More than just a song to sing,
C#m7
More than words and offerings;
F#m7
We need Your presence more than an - ything.

CHANNEL:

A2 C#m7 Bsus
And You're all that we want, You're all that we need.
A2 C#m7 Bsus
You're all that we want, You're all that we need.

(repeat CHORUS)

VERSE 3:

C#m7 F#m7
You call us closer to Your heart;
C#m7
Lead us, Lord, to where You are.
F#m7
We need Your presence more than an - ything.

(repeat CHANNEL and CHORUS)

CHANNEL 2:

F#m7 E/G#
And You're all that we want, You're all that we need.
A2 C#m7 Bsus
You're all that we want, You're all that we need.

(repeat CHORUS)

A2
We know where the Spirit of the Lord is.
C#m7 Bsus
Where the Spirit of the Lord is, there is liberty.

(repeat 3x)

A2 C#m7 Bsus

A2 C#m7 Bsus

A2

Rise and Sing

STEVE FEE

KEY OF (B)

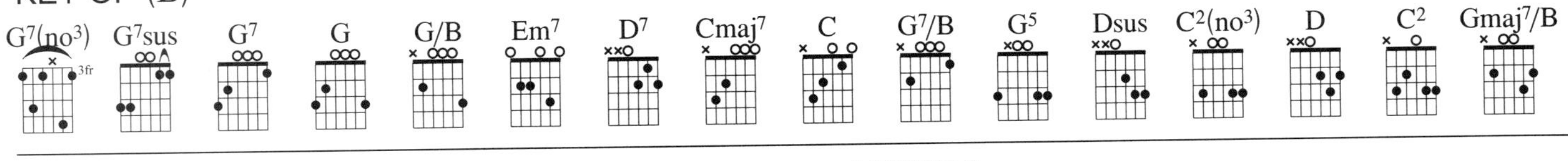

Capo 4th fret (G)

$G^7(no^3)$ G^7sus G^7 G^7sus

G G/B Em^7 D^7 $Cmaj^7$

G G/B Em^7 D^7 $Cmaj^7$

VERSE 1:

$G^7(no^3)$ C
If you're alive and you've been redeemed,
G^7/B C
Rise and sing, rise and sing.
$G^7(no^3)$ C
If you've been touched by the Mercy King,
G^7/B C
Rise and sing, rise and sing.
G^5
Woh woh. Woh woh.

VERSE 2:

G^7/B C
If you were bound but now you're free,
G^7/B C
Rise and sing, rise and sing.
G^7/B C
Lift up a shout of vic - tory,
G^7/B C
Rise and sing, rise and sing.
G^5
Woh woh. Woh woh.

CHORUS:

G G/B
Our God is risen and reigning,
Em^7 Dsus $C^2(no^3)$
And we're ele - vating
G G/B Em^7
The glory of our God and King. * ****(repeat from here)***
D N.C. G
Everybody rise and sing.
G/B Em^7 D^7 $Cmaj^7$

VERSE 3:

G^7/B C
If in your heart rings a melody,
G^7/B C
Rise and sing, rise and sing.
G^7/B C
If you have tasted and you have seen,
G^7/B C
Rise and sing, rise and sing.
G^5
Woh woh. Woh woh.

(repeat CHORUS)

BRIDGE:

G^5 D C^2
Let the redeemed of the Lord sing, "Hallelujah!"
G^5 D C^2
Let the redeemed of the Lord sing, "Our God reigns!"
G^5 G/B
Let the redeemed of the Lord sing,
Em^7 Dsus C^2
"Hallelu - jah!" ("Hallelu - jah!)
G^5 $Gmaj^7/B$
Let the redeemed of the Lord sing,
Em^7 Dsus C^2
"Our God reigns!" ("Our God reigns!")
G^5 G/B
Let the redeemed of the Lord sing,
Em^7 Dsus C^2
"Hallelu - jah!" ("Hallelu - jah!)
G^5 $Gmaj^7/B$
Let the redeemed of the Lord sing,
Em^7 Dsus N.C. Dsus N.C.
"Our God reigns!" ("Our God reigns!")

(repeat CHORUS 2x)

N.C. G

Like a Lion

DANIEL BASHTA

KEY OF (G#m)

Em7 D G Dsus Am7 C D(add4) G2 Dsus/F#

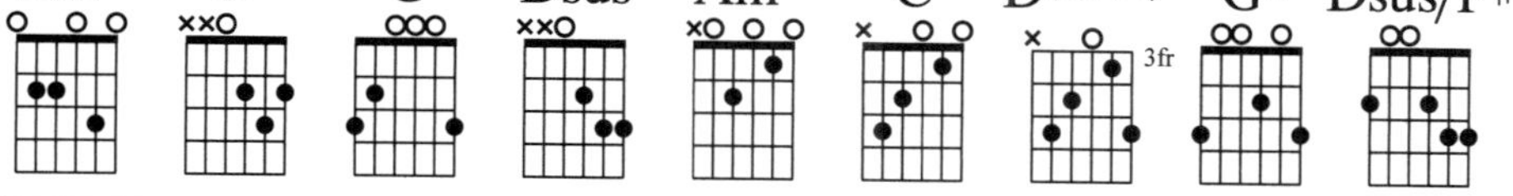

Capo 4th fret (Em)

Em7 D G Em7 D G

(repeat 3x)

VERSE 1:

Em7 Dsus G
Let love ex - plode, and bring the dead to life;
Am7 G C
A love so bold to see a revo - lution somehow.

(repeat)

CHANNEL:

D(add4) Em7
Now I'm lost in Your free - dom;
D(add4) C
Oh, this world I'll overcome.

CHORUS:

D N.C.*
My God's not dead, He's surely alive;
Em7
And he's liv - ing on the inside, roaring like a lion.
D(add4)
My God's not dead, He's surely alive;
Em7
And he's liv - ing on the inside, roaring like a lion.

****(if CHORUS is repeated back to back, don't play the stop)***

Em7 D G

VERSE 2:

Em7 Dsus G
Let hope a - rise, and make the darkness hide.
Am7 G C
My faith is dead; I need a resur - rection somehow.

(repeat)

CONTINUED...

(repeat CHANNEL, repeat CHORUS 2x)

G2 Dsus/F#

Em7 C
He's surely alive! Oh, He's surely alive!

BRIDGE:

G2 Dsus/F#
Let heaven roar and fire fall;
Em7 Am7
Come shake the ground with the sound of re - vival.

(repeat 4x)

(repeat CHORUS 2x)

Em7 D

G Em7 D
Oh, He's surely alive! Oh, He's surely alive!
G Em7 D
Oh, He's surely alive! Oh, He's surely alive!
G Em7 D
Oh, He's surely alive, yeah!
G

Chosen Generation

CHRIS TOMLIN, LOUIE GIGLIO, DANIEL CARSON, and JESSE REEVES

KEY OF (B)

G^2 G^2/B Em^7 $C^2(no^3)$ $A^{7(add4)}$ $Am^{7(4)}$

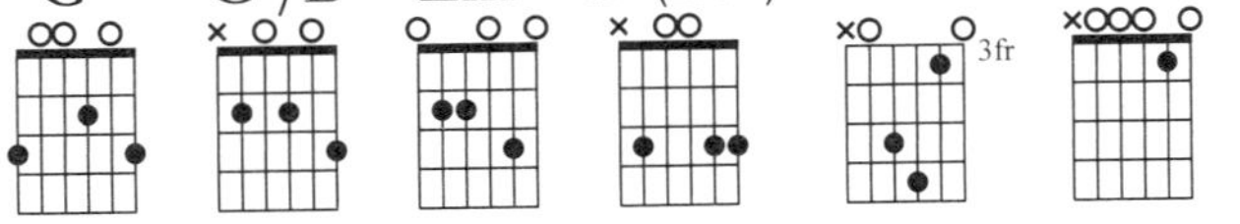

Capo 4th fret (G)

G^2 G^2/B Em^7 $C^2(no^3)$

CHORUS:

G^2 G^2/B
We are a chosen gener - ation,
Em^7 $C^2(no^3)$
Rise up, Holy nation; God, we live for You.
G^2 G^2/B
You have called us out of darkness
Em^7 $C^2(no^3)$
Into light so glorious; God, we live for You,

*(We live for You, God, we live for You.)

****(1st x only)***

VERSE:

$C^2(no^3)$ G^2/B G^2
We run with passion for Your name, we run.
$C^2(no^3)$ G^2/B G^2
Free - dom, You've broken every chain, we run.
$C^2(no^3)$
And our God will not be moved;
G^2
Our God will never be shaken.
$A^{7(add4)}$ $C^2(no^3)$
We run to You, we run!

(repeat CHORUS, VERSE, and CHORUS)

$C^2(no^3)$ N.C.
And our God will not be moved;

Our God will never be shaken.

And our God will not be moved;

Our God will never be shaken.

$C^2(no^3)$
And our God will not be moved;
G^2/B G^2
Our God will never be shaken.
$A^{7(add4)}$ $C^2(no^3)$
We run to You, we run!

(repeat CHORUS)

BRIDGE:

G^2 $C^2(no^3)$
You are everything, more than all we need;
G^2/B $Am^{7(4)}$
God, we live for You, God, we live for You.
G^2 $C^2(no^3)$
I found this world to be not e - nough for me.
G^2/B $Am^{7(4)}$
God, we live for You, God, we live for You.
G^2 $C^2(no^3)$ G^2/B $Am^{7(4)}$

(repeat CHORUS 2x)

We live for You, God, we live for You.

With Everything

JOEL HOUSTON

KEY OF (B)

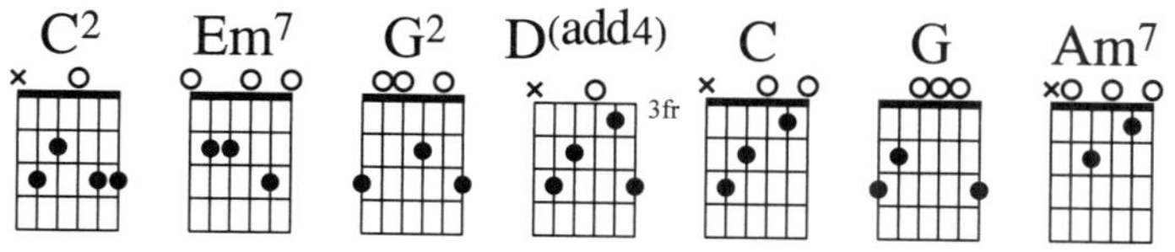

Capo 4th fret (G)

VERSE:

C2 Em7 G2
Name above names, Lamb that was slain;
D(add4)
A beautiful God.
C2 Em7 G2
The King above kings, God of all things;
D(add4)
A beautiful God.

CHANNEL:

C2 Em7
And there is no other name
G2 D(add4)
Like Je - sus.
C2 Em7
We give You all of the praise,
G2 D(add4)
O Lord, Je - sus.

CHORUS 1:

Em7 C G
So let hope rise,
D(add4) Em7 C G
And darkness tremble in Your holy light
D(add4) Em7 C G
That every eye will see Jesus, our God,
D(add4) C D(add4)
Great and mighty to be praised.

CHORUS 2:

Em7 C G
So let hope rise,
D(add4) Em7 C G
And darkness tremble in Your holy light
D(add4) C2 Em7 D(add4)
That every eye will see Jesus, our God,
Am7 C2 D(add4)
Great and mighty to be praised.

BRIDGE:

G2
God of all days,
D(add4) Em7
Glorious in all of Your ways;
C2 G2
The majesty, the wonder, and grace
D(add4) Em7 C2
In the light of Your name.

(repeat CHORUS 2)

C Em7 G D(add4)

BREAKDOWN:

C Em7
With ev - erything, with ev - erything,
G D(add4)
We will shout for Your glo - ry.
C Em7
With ev - erything, with ev - erything,
G D(add4)
We will shout forth Your praise.

(repeat)

C2 Em7
Our hearts, they cry, "Be glo - rified!
G2 D(add4)
Be lift - ed high above all!"
C2 Em7
For You, our King, with ev - erything,
G2 D(add4)
We will shout forth Your praise!

OUTRO:

C Em7 G D(add4)
Woah woah woah
C Em7 G D(add4)
Woah woah woah
(repeat OUTRO as desired, with variation)
C2

awaken
my
heart